A SEAT AT THE TABLE

A SEAT AT THE TABLE

THE MAKING OF BUSBOYS AND POETS

ANDY SHALLAL

O/R

OR Books

New York · London

Published by OR Books, New York and London
Visit our website at www.orbooks.com

All rights information: rights@orbooks.com

First printing 2025
Cataloging-in-Publication data is available from the Library of Congress.
A catalog record for this book is available from the British Library.

Typeset by Lapiz Digital Services. Printed by BookMobile, USA, and CPI, UK.
Cover photo by Dwayne Gayle

Hardback ISBN 9781682196380 • E-book 9781682196397

This book is dedicated to my wife and life partner Marjan

CONTENTS

FOREWORD

Andy Shallal's fascinating memoir is being published precisely at a time when the story of Busboys and Poets – its advocacy of radical community-building in support of struggles for justice throughout the world, combined with its insistence on deep intellectual, aesthetic, and culinary communion – is more relevant and more needed than ever. Over the last twenty years, Shallal and his impressive collection of eight venues that combine restaurant, bookstore, and performance space have played an especially crucial role inside the nation's capital, a city that likes to imagine itself as the most important geographical site on the globe – perhaps even in the universe.

As *A Seat at the Table* goes to press, Gaza continues to be the target of a devastating, ongoing genocide, daily enacted and regularly escalated by the Israeli Defense Force. But, at the same time, and thanks to the consistent work of Busboys and other progressive formations across the country, this is the very first time that we have experienced such expansive and spirited solidarity with Palestine. As we grieve the devastating death and destruction in Gaza, we are also reminded by the visual art, poetry, and other modes of cultural and political resistance promoted by Busboys that the genocidal tragedy we have watched for more than a year is being actively opposed by increasing numbers of people throughout the world. And this itself is the harbinger of increased global possibilities for justice, equality, and peace.

The fact that, as the name of a restaurant and cultural center, the phrase "busboys and poets" now resonates so widely is a testament not only to his impressive artistic and culinary abilities, but also to the prescience and dedication of Andy Shallal. Thanks to him, new generations have been introduced to the life and works of busboy and poet Langston Hughes, for whom these community institutions are named. When I first learned about Andy's dedication to the memory of Langston Hughes and, like Hughes, to the cause of global liberation, I felt an instant affinity with him. As a revolutionary poet who challenged racism and defended the rights of workers everywhere, Hughes has had a lasting impact on my own life, beginning the first time I heard him speak before a Black audience in Birmingham, Alabama when I was a small child.

I did not actually meet the person who was introducing Langston Hughes to new generations and whose brainchild became a not-to-be-missed D.C. institution until Andy Shallal himself invited me to participate in the 2013 Peace Ball coinciding with the second Obama Inauguration. While the first Obama victory, regardless of one's political critiques, was a world historical event, celebrated on every continent, the second victory did not occasion dancing in the streets...but rather left many of us as skeptical about bourgeois democracy as we had always been. So when I was invited by Andy to the Peace Ball that year, I had my usual misgivings about celebrating someone who had proven himself more than capable of generating support among major players in global capitalism. But Andy had accumulated more than enough experiences in radical movement organizing to steer himself away from the myopic political visions promoted by conventional electoral politics, and the many Peace Ball programs over the years have emphasized a collective vision that is broad, encompassing, and reflective of a long-term commitment to global peace and justice that transcends any particular political administration. *A Seat at the Table* reveals the depth of this commitment and allows us to understand how Andy's continued support of artists, poets, and writers, and his and Busboy's facilitation of community-based movement-building, exemplifies what we can all do to continue to safeguard radical democratic possibilities for our worlds. In this particular moment, that commitment will be more important than ever.

— ANGELA Y. DAVIS

PREFACE

It didn't take long for me to realize that Busboys and Poets was a special place. It crackled and buzzed from its first opening night back in September 2005. With the Iraq war in full force and the streets on fire with activists and anti-war protestors, the timing could not have been more fortuitous.

When I set out to write this book I had no idea what the arc of the story would be. I wasn't sure whether to make it about Busboys and Poets itself, or about my journey starting as an 11-year-old coming to America and discovering a world as foreign as a distant planet. I settled on telling my story from the time I arrived in America to the opening of Busboys and Poets. In it, I try to get the reader to understand the inflection points that led me to take on such a project. I cannot tell you how often people ask me how I came up with this idea. My answer is always simple: It's not the idea that is unique but rather the synergy of the various aspects of Busboys and Poets. It is first and foremost a restaurant. But it is also a bar, a lounge, a gathering space with free Wi-Fi, a poetry venue, a stage for political and cultural discussions, and a venue for music and art. At the entrance is a bookstore with carefully curated titles dealing with a variety of social justice issues as well as literature and poetry. Busboys and Poets is a place where you can take a deliberate pause to dream, to think, to nourish your body, to meet a friend or take in an unexpected program or a poetry open mic, to write the next great American novel, or just to chill.

So much has happened in the 19 years since the first Busboys and Poets opened its doors. Incredible events that I have reflected on and cherished. The night with Howard Zinn is surely one to remember. It was merely months after opening. I remember the line forming hours before his appearance. By the time he arrived, it was at least two blocks long. Then there was the evening with Octavia Butler, the great sci-fi author. It was Halloween 2005. We had only been open for a little over a month. She sat on the Langston Room stage in a throne-like chair, surrounded by candles and a smoke machine to add a spooky touch. Her reading would be one of the last readings before she died tragically from a fall at her home in Seattle just months later.

There are so many memorable nights with some of the most important writers and literary activists of our time: Alice Walker, Angela Davis, Nikki Giovanni, Ethelbert Miller, Sonia Sanchez and a host of others.

In telling this story, I have left out some significant chunks of my life and changed some names to protect privacy. I also made some slight compressions of timelines to better connect some of the chapters. But everything is factually correct as I recall it and none of the omissions have an impact on the overall story. I hope you enjoy reading it as much as I enjoyed writing it.

—ANDY SHALLAL
Washington, DC, November, 2024

PROLOGUE

HAVING A BALL

The crowd inside Busboys and Poets arrived throughout the afternoon. Many were wearing "I voted" stickers. It was November 4, 2008, presidential election night, and Busboys and Poets, having been open merely two years, was already the go-to place for progressives in DC and beyond. That year, the *Washington City Paper*'s annual People's Choice Awards had named Busboys "The Best Place to Take an Out of Towner," beating out the National Mall and the National Gallery of Art. When I read that, it brought a huge smile to my face. "It doesn't get bigger than this," I thought.

Election night is the Super Bowl for political junkies, and that evening, Busboys and Poets was ground zero. It was the sort of occasion Busboys and Poets was made for. It's a place where art, culture and politics intentionally collide. Communal settings with couches and coffee tables are scattered throughout the space, encouraging strangers to interact with one another organically. A well-sourced menu, heavy with vegetarian and vegan options, caters to almost every whim. At the entrance is a bookstore with a selection of books dealing with history, social justice, literature and poetry. More than a restaurant, Busboys and Poets is a hangout, a watering hole, a place where someone can take a deliberate pause and linger for hours feeding their mind, body and soul.

This particular election was especially consequential. It was a watershed moment for many activists, me included. As a hyphenated American, I felt an added obligation to prove to the world and to myself that we were better than what had come before. The previous eight years of the George W. Bush presidency had been exhausting. They were full of lies and deception and wars thousands of miles away, including in my birthplace, Iraq. They were the years of The Patriot Act, legalized torture and the Guantanamo Bay prison filled with Muslim men, hooded and languishing in cages. One of them could have been a friend, an uncle, a relative. These were also the years of Abu Ghraib and Falluja and the "Axis of Evil." Places that I was familiar with. My family used to have picnics on the banks of the Euphrates in Falluja. Now it was remembered for something unspeakable.

Suddenly, apparently out of nowhere, Barack Obama appeared. His message was one of hope and change. An out of the box candidate who miraculously seemed able to channel people's anxiety and frustration into the ballot box. I remember being in the Langston Room at Busboys and Poets for a gathering that had been organized to watch his announcement from Springfield, Illinois, that he intended to run for president. It was a bone cold Saturday morning in February 2007. Some people had arrived early to get a booth close to the screen and enjoy a mimosa and a leisurely brunch. That morning, the room was pulsating with energy. A crush of mostly young hipsters huddled inside, forcing the doors to stay open to allow for the overflow of people craning to get a view of the large screen. There were diehards among the group, but mostly it was made up of curious bystanders wanting to learn more about this Black man who was defying all odds to throw his hat into the ring. At that time, I knew little about this new senator from Illinois. My only in-person encounter was having sat next to him at a

Congressional Black Caucus Dinner. That night he said very little and seemed somewhat cagy and aloof. There was nothing extraordinary about him from what I could recollect.

As Obama finished his announcement speech, I could see that people were already smitten and ready to roll up their sleeves and get to work on his behalf. The bandwagon was well underway, and I hopped on. I went to work immediately: volunteering, raising money, making calls, whatever it took. And for the next few months, getting Obama elected became an obsession. I had the zealotry of a disciple.

At Busboys and Poets in the months ahead, we held too many fundraisers to count, raising tens of thousands of dollars for the campaign. Obama himself didn't show up, that wouldn't happen until his second term, but we had a plethora of surrogates come through, including Susan Rice, Tom Daschle and Jesse Jackson. Before or since, I never worked so hard on an election. I even rented a couple of buses and took more than 100 volunteers for a day of campaigning in Columbus, Ohio. It was a 24-hour sleepless whirlwind and I felt great doing it. Marjan, my wife, was all in too. She recruited friends in Virginia and spent weeks doing lit drops and knocking on doors convincing people to vote for Obama. She was relentless and worked to the very last night before the election, staying out till the wee hours distributing door hangers to remind people to vote the next day. I remember her calling me around 1 a.m. on the eve of the election to report that they were trespassing into people's yards and hoping they didn't get shot. My wife is not an adventurous person, but getting Obama elected was a calling.

When it comes to politics, I'm not one who easily succumbs to sentimentality. However, Election Day 2008 still brings goose bumps and a lump in my throat. I can remember, as if I was still there, the evening we gathered at Busboys to watch the results coming in: the black "good luck" turtleneck sweater I wore; the wireless microphone I used to announce state-by-state results as they filtered through; the cheering crowd and the nervousness in the room when the results were too close to call or tipped the other way; the groups of friends at the edge of their seats.

As the night wore on, the atmosphere became still more tense. The election was closer than anyone wanted it to be. By then the place was so jammed it was nearly impossible to move. Service came to a halt, and everyone held their breath. When the words "Obama Elected President of the United States" splashed across all four screens, everyone jumped up and screamed. You could feel the collective joy. People were hugging, high fiving, blowing kisses at complete strangers. Some had little American flags at the ready. Several people openly wept. Earlier that night I had cued the song "Celebrate" by Kool & the Gang for what I hoped would be the moment of victory. I cranked up the music and the place descended into mayhem. People took the celebration to the street. The traffic at the corner of 14th and U Street came to a standstill. Horns were blowing continuously. Some people started a conga line that spanned several blocks. I even saw a drag queen in a full sequined gown sitting on a convertible waving to the crowd like Miss America. Revelers poured out from apartments and restaurants and bars. Nobody wanted to experience this moment alone.

It took a while for things to settle down that night and I don't remember going to sleep. But when I woke up, I picked up that day's edition of the *Washington Post*. There it was in a huge headline: OBAMA MAKES HISTORY with a front-page photograph of his family on stage, smiling and waving to well-wishers in a Chicago ballroom. Michelle and the two daughters looked radiant. This was no dream, it was real. Suddenly, the eight years of Bush/Cheney seemed light-years away. Now it was all about hope and change and good things ahead. Below the fold of the newspaper was another large photo. This one was of a group of Black women with a hand-ful of men behind them. Tears were streaming down the women's faces and the men were cupping their mouths with their hands, standing there in disbelief. The photo became an icon of Obama's victory. It was taken at Busboys and Poets. Not at the 14th and V location where I had spent most of the night, but at the 5th and K location, where the NAACP under the leadership of Ben Jealous had rented the entire restaurant. Their party became ground zero for a who's who of Black leadership, including members of Congress who streamed in and out throughout the night. The article that accompanied the photo began with a mention of Busboys and Poets. I was ecstatic. I ran out to the nearest 7-Eleven with the intention of buying as many copies of the paper as I could lay my hands on. But even though it was only 8 a.m., the newspaper stand was already empty. People knew that day's paper would become a collector's item and were buying multiple copies.

I dashed home, quickly dressed, and headed to the restaurant to meet with the management team to assess the previous night. We shared the highlights: how quickly the place had filled up, the line that serpentined for an entire block. The excitement when the results came in. Nobody wanted the moment to end. We even toyed with the idea of an afterparty. Then a thought sprang to my mind and I blurted it out: "Why don't we organize a big ball to mark the inauguration? We could call it 'The Peace Ball.'"

Balls had never attracted me much; I'd never even attended one. They seemed too posh and phony. Not exactly on brand for Busboys and Poets. However, this time seemed different. It was a moment that crystallized what Busboys and Poets was all about.

I decided to run the idea past a few people I respected and trusted. Howard Zinn was my first call. I had gotten to know

Howard over the years and wanted to hear his thoughts. To me, he was the grandfather of progressive ideas and someone who would give legitimacy to such an unconventional event. I asked if he would consider being the honorary host for the evening.

Howard laughed and took a deep breath.

"Andy, you seem very excited about this, but I want to remind you that Obama is a politician and as such he will disappoint you."

I don't remember precisely how I responded, but it was something to the effect of, maybe this time it would be different.

After some serious arm twisting, Howard was on board, He made clear his agreement was less about celebrating Obama's win and more about appeasing me. With the honorary host secured, I proceeded to make phone calls to bring on others. Within days, our roster included heavy hitters such as Harry Belafonte, Alice Walker, Jackson Browne, Angelique Kidjo, Michael Franti, Joan Baez and Eve Ensler. We secured the National Postal Museum for the venue, hired an events coordinator and put together a promotional campaign, which turned out to be superfluous: The Peace Ball sold out within a week. People who had never been to a ball, progressives looking to extend the election night euphoria, peace activists and Busboys and Poets fans rushed to make reservations, and for the next two months I spent most of my time avoiding phone calls from people begging for a ticket. We soon had 1,600 people coming to a venue with a legal capacity of 1,000. On the night of the ball, my fingers were crossed that no one was keeping count.

Due to heightened security, those who were lucky enough to get a ticket had to park blocks away and brave the icy wind. Once inside, however, the room radiated with warmth and an energy that made you forget the polar temperatures outside. Bars were placed throughout, serving champagne and cocktails, and we set up a long buffet laden with salads and skewered meats. A jazz band lent the night an appropriate elegance. Long evening gowns and tuxedos mingled with fashionable jeans and sloganed t-shirts. Peace signs were everywhere, in keeping with the theme. One attendee even had their braided hair made into a peace sign above their head. Everything and everyone sparkled.

Joan Baez opened the show with a performance of John Lennon's "Imagine." The crowd went crazy when she walked onto the stage, guitar slung across her shoulder. For many there, she represented a legacy of activism that had altered the course of history and a link from the past to the present. Hers was a tough act to follow but those appearing next made it look easy: Harry, Eve, Alice and so many others. The evening was capped with a rousing finale by the wonderful Angelique Kidjo, who brought the crowd to their feet, their arms in the air, waving in unison. The die had been re-cast. Busboys and Poets had shown that it was more than a restaurant with a progressive twist. It was the tent under which the peace movement could gather to celebrate, to dance, to rejoice and re-energize.

I stood on the corner of the stage behind Kidjo, looking across the ornate Postal Museum with its soaring columns washed in purple lights, carved ceiling, brass chandeliers and marble floor, framing a rich tapestry of people, Black, white, brown, young and old, dancing and laughing together. It was a spectacle that made Busboys and Poets' three-year journey, beginning with our opening day in 2005, all the more worthwhile. Gone were the days where progressives had to meet in church basements, or school gymnasiums, sitting on metal folding chairs, under fluorescent lights, eating cold pizza and drinking soda. Movements can exact a toll on one's physical and mental health. Burnout has caused many to ditch activism and take up organic farming or check out altogether.

I wanted to create a place that was unabashedly progressive. A place with a core mission to bring together people who believe a better world is possible, and to do so in a joyful way. I recalled what Emma Goldman, the early 20th century anarchist said in her autobiography about being an activist:

> At the dances I was one of the most untiring and gayest. One evening a cousin of Sasha, a young boy, took me aside. With a grave face, as if he were about to announce the death of a dear comrade, he whispered to me that it did not behoove an agitator to dance. Certainly not with such reckless abandon, anyway. It was undignified for one who was on the way to becoming a force in the anarchist movement. My frivolity would only hurt the Cause. I grew furious at the impudent interference of the boy. I told him to mind his own business. I was tired of having the Cause constantly thrown into my face. I did not believe that a Cause which stood for a beautiful ideal, for anarchism, for release and freedom from convention and prejudice, should demand the denial of life and joy. I insisted that our Cause could not expect me to become a nun and that the movement would not be turned into a cloister. If it meant that, I did not want it.

With the rhythmic drumbeat and brass sounds echoing across the ceiling of the museum and the jubilant crowd below, I came off the stage and joined the throng. By the time the music died, it was well past midnight. I was exhausted, soaked with sweat, and wrapped in the glow of the night, thinking that maybe, just maybe, this time a revolution was looming ahead and I was thrilled to be playing a part in it.

1

MY NAME IS ANAS

My story begins in the fall of 1966. That was the year my family came to America. I was eleven and America seemed as distant as the furthest star in the sky. I never imagined in a million years that coming here was an option. Until then, I had only known of the United States through watching television back in Baghdad, the city where I was born and the place that I continue to call home.

That summer my father was offered a position to represent the Arab League in Washington, DC. Back then, the Arab League was something. Headquartered in Cairo, it was an organization meant to unite the Arab World. A futile effort becoming still more distant in the years ahead. The League had offices all over the world: Bonn, Paris, London and the most coveted one, Washington, DC. My father got the job by sheer luck. It happened over a vacation encounter with someone high up in the League's bureaucracy, who also happened to know my father. Within an hour over coffee and several cigarettes on the open terrace of the Splendid Hotel in the mountains of Lebanon, the offer was made. My father quickly accepted, and our lives would change forever. Within days we were aboard a first-class flight on Swiss Air heading to America.

As we arrived at National Airport, my uncle Suham was waiting for us along with a cluster of friends, a handful of officials from the Iraqi embassy and one or two people my parents knew from before. I had not seen my uncle for years but soon spotted him standing at the front of the small group of well-dressed men and women. He was easy to pick out. Dark and stocky with a thick head of fine hair. He was in his thirties but looked older and frumpier than I remembered. I had forgotten that he lived here, and I was happy to see a familiar face in a sea of strangers. He had come to America to study international law at George Washington University and, like most Iraqis who studied abroad, he never went back.

"Anas? Look at how dark you are!" These were the first words out of my uncle's mouth the minute he saw me.

"Anas, habibi, why are you so dark?" he repeated with a pitiful tone. "You must have been in the sun a lot?"

I was stunned and just stood there hoping to disappear. Then he turned to my father, "Why do you let him out in the sun so much?"

Facing me again, he ran his hand across the top of my head.

"Look at your hair! Where did you get this wool? I am sure people will think you are Black. You should not play in the sun. Be careful! Americans don't like Black people, you will see. Be careful."

His machine-gun barrage continued.

"They call Black people negroes," he said, stretching the word "negroes," and then he gave out a big laugh.

Returning his gaze to my father, he said with genuine concern, "You won't be able to go to many places, you will see!" My face turned red, my eyes brimmed with tears, embarrassment and shame washed over me. I wanted to turn around and go back to Baghdad.

On the drive to the hotel, my thoughts eventually turned to the world around me. Rows of trees lined the sides of the road. I had never seen so many trees. We arrived just as the sun was dipping behind Rock Creek Park, the lengthening rays streaming through the thick green foliage. In Baghdad, trees were few and far between. You could go for hundreds of meters without spotting one. I inhaled deeply air that was delightfully fresh. I took note of how clean and orderly the city was. The smooth roads with clear yellow and white stripes. The traffic lights at every major intersection.

My father struck up a conversation with the driver, showing off his English. I sat in the backseat with my older brother and younger sister and watched a dazzling new world roll by. I couldn't believe my dream of coming to America was real, and I resented my uncle for spoiling it.

Our destination was The Windsor Park Hotel, which would be our home for the next few days. It sat at the top of a hill overlooking the edge of the park, part of a quiet enclave of embassy residences, expensive homes, and apartment buildings with well-kept gardens.

Our stay at The Windsor Park was short-lived and soon we moved into a three-bedroom ground-floor apartment with a sliding glass door that led into an open grassy area overlooking a large parking lot and a pool where we would spend every waking hour during the summer months, despite my uncle's warning. My older brother, Yasir, and I shared a bedroom. It was minimally furnished with two twin beds separated by a small nightstand. I took the bed closer to the window. My brother, the one closer to the door. The other bedroom was my sister Suhair's, which she would be sharing with our soon-to-be-born baby sister, May. The kitchen was a narrow galley with brown and beige speckled Formica counters on both sides and barely enough room for one person to pass through. In the middle of the living room sat the TV, which became my window into American culture, where I learned most of my English.

The Northern Virginia location was convenient for my father—a mere 20-minute drive from the Arab League office in Dupont Circle. My Uncle had advised us to move there, telling my parents that the schools in Virginia were much better than the ones in DC. "There are fewer Black people in Virginia," he said. "It's much safer here."

On the morning of my first school day in America, two weeks after leaving my life in Baghdad and just one day after moving into our apartment, I stood in front of the mirror in the one bathroom my siblings and I shared, and I did not like what I saw. My uncle's words continued to gnaw at me. My woolly hair, my brown skin, and the sun blotches on my face had suddenly become more pronounced.

I sprinkled water on my hair and pressed it down, parting it with both hands, trying to straighten it. I ran a comb through it to smooth it further. I tried hot water and a hot towel, which scalded my hands and only made my hair frizzier. Nothing seemed to work. With time running out, I quickly put on the black pants and the white shirt that I ironed the night before. I wanted to make a good first impression. I was envious of my brother who appeared to be less concerned about these things and took just minutes to get ready. He looked Caucasian and was often mistaken for Italian or Greek with his lighter skin, wavy hair, and thin lips. Unlike me, he had little trouble fitting in.

My brother and I followed my father out the sliding door onto the sidewalk. We walked past the parking lot and the swimming pool and headed to the tunnel beneath the highway that led to the school just a few hundred meters away. Around us, groups of kids were funneling in. Some did double takes as they passed us, taking note of the three unfamiliar strangers. My father, tall and dark, stood out. A smoldering cigarette dangled from his lips and made him squint. The school was a two-story, red brick structure with dark green doors. An expansive football field that doubled as a sledding playground during the winter took up most of the space on one side of the building. A large oak tree with a halo of colorful leaves gave shade to the entrance. Inside, past the open atrium of the lobby, the hallway pulsated. We weaved our way to the office. Past the kids bumping, laughing and huddling amongst themselves, and finally making our way through the echoing thunder of lockers. Once inside the school office, things suddenly got much quieter.

Straight ahead we were faced with a high counter, where teachers, parents and kids vied for attention. All around, the walls were filled with bulletin boards plastered with notes that I was unable to make out. People rushed in and out. Teachers milled about. A large woman with screaming red lipstick and a pale face framed by a helmet of coal black hair approached my father. My brother and I waited. Once in a while, I caught a stare that made me self-conscious, causing me to smooth my hair with my hands and slouch in my seat.

In the meantime, my father was cutting a deal with the principal. Somehow, he convinced him that I should begin in eighth grade despite the fact I was only eleven. "Anas is a very good student. He can memorize anything very fast," my father told the principal. He came fully prepared with transcripts and recommendations from my teachers and principals back in Baghdad. My older brother was not given the accelerated option for practical reasons. My parents apparently thought having both of us eventually catch up to one another would be useful. For one thing we would share the same car going to and from school.

Moments later, a skinny boy wearing shorts with thick blond hair and stick legs—my designated school guide—walked in and stood before me looking as if he had a gun held to his head. The helmet lady came from behind the counter and introduced him to me as Michael. He had bangs that hovered over his eyes like a visor and every few seconds he jerked his head to one side, to clear his vision.

"Michael," the woman said. "I want you to meet Anus." At her pronunciation of my name, his face suddenly lit up. "Hi," he said, with a grin, as if awakened from a slumber.

As we walked out of the office, I gave my father and my brother a goodbye look and followed the kid into the hallway, trailing close behind. "What's your name again?" he asked, making sure he didn't miss it.

"My name is Anas," I said.

He smiled again, this time showing more teeth and a slight chuckle. "Anus?" he repeated. I smiled back, nodding my head approvingly, unaware of the trap I had walked into. We made several turns, finally finding our way to my locker. When we arrived, he handed me a piece of paper with a series of numbers.

"This is the combination to your locker, Anus," he said. "Let me show you. First you turn it clockwise and then counterclockwise and then back again. Do you have any questions, Anus?"

I was delighted at his sudden friendliness. When we were done, he deposited me in front of my first period class.

"Bye, Anus," he said, loud enough for everyone to hear, while waving.

"Goodbye," I said, waving back.

Everyone sniggered.

After that I didn't see him for the rest of the day, and I had no idea how to find my locker, let alone open it. I couldn't find my classes either, and for the first few days of Stratford Junior High, I often wandered the halls, lost, well after the bell rang.

Eventually someone, a teacher, a kind student, or a custodian would relay me to the office for assistance.

During those days, walking the hallways in middle school was like auditioning for a part without a script. It took me a while to make sense of things, even to figure out why my name seemed so funny. In the hallways, kids would greet me each time they passed, repeating my name over and over. "Hey, Anus," one would shout from a distance. "Good morning, Anus," another one would call out enthusiastically. Even the teachers were in on the joke. They just stood by idly.

At first, I was thrilled, thinking Americans were so welcoming. When it became obvious that something was afoot, I looked up the word "Anas" in the dictionary. "Anas: the Latin word for duck, Anas platyrhynchos." I accepted my fate as a duck, which didn't seem that bad, until one day it was revealed to me what the fuss was all about. A girl named Gail, who felt sorry for me, pulled me aside to break the news, which she did without laughing or even smiling.

"A-n-u-s is a bad word," she spelled it out, trying to explain it to me delicately.

"That isn't my name," I said. "My name is A-n-a-s, not A-n-u-s."

By then it was too late. There was no way of fighting it. I was devastated and ready to drop out. The best I could do then was avoid the ringleaders.

Stuff was coming at me from all directions. Once, during the first week, I was stopped by a girl in the hallway. She wore a pleated skirt that was a few inches above her chubby knees, and her skin was the color of dark polished wood. "Are you high yellow?" she asked, and then she giggled and ran back to her group of friends. I smiled and turned red as a pomegranate. I didn't know what "high yellow" meant and was afraid to ask. Embarrassed, I walked away quietly, wondering if being "high yellow" was a good thing or not.

When I got home, I took to the dictionary once again but couldn't find anything that made sense. The two words were not connected in any way. I didn't know whom to ask and I opted to keep it to myself. In the short time since coming to America, I had already started to notice differences in how people looked all around me. On the street. In the grocery store. And now here at school where everything seemed more defined. I began to take note of who sat together during lunch. The huddles in the hallways and after school. The kids walking home. There was little racial mixing that I could see. I suspected that perhaps the girl in the pleated skirt wanted to know if I was one of them.

Then there was gym period, where people got naked in public. I mean completely naked, running around with penises flopping and balls dangling. I was dumbfounded. They took showers together. Total strangers. Why didn't anyone warn me about this? These kids had pubes. At eleven, my testicles hadn't even dropped yet. I refused to take my clothes off and compete with kids that were a lot older than I was. Instead, I wiped the few drops of sweat I had on my body with a towel and dressed very quickly facing my locker. This went on for a few days until Mr. Graham noticed that I was not showering. He told me that I had to and threw a towel my way.

"How old are you anyway?" he asked.

"Eleven," I said sheepishly.

"Oh," he said, bewildered at the answer. "This is eighth grade," he added, wondering if I was lost or had gotten there by mistake.

I just smiled.

He shook his head and simply walked away, leaving me standing with a towel in my hand. I quickly wrapped the towel around my body and bolted in and out of the shower as fast as humanly possible. In the days to come, I would skip showering whenever I thought Mr. Graham was not watching.

My favorite class by far was Mrs. Golden's art class and it became my refuge during my first year at Stratford Junior High. It was full of bins with colored paper, yarn, glue, jars of paint and brushes and colored pencils. It was art Shangri-La. Best of all, art class didn't require speaking. It was the only class I looked forward to. Art class made going to school bearable that first year. Art was something I knew I was good at. I found this out when I was eight. A friend of my mother gave me a crayon coloring set and construction paper for my birthday. I couldn't wait to open the box of colors. I dropped to the floor and just went at it. I must have colored for hours. I drew a pond with ducks and a mountain range on the horizon. I have no idea where I had seen such an image. There was no mountain range anywhere near Baghdad. My mother did a double take as she passed by. "Did you do this?" she asked. "Yes." I said. I was so excited she had noticed. My mother is not a gusher. But on that day, having witnessed my first "masterpiece," she was gushing.

It was no secret that, during those early days at Stratford, it was mostly doom and gloom with an occasional flicker of hope. Gail became my hero and a friend, correcting their pronunciation whenever someone mentioned my name. "Look shorty, find someone your own size to pick on. Oh, I forgot there is no one your size!" she once told a short, snarky kid who was making fun of my name. She wasn't particularly menacing, just loaded with smart quips. She was one of my few true friends in middle school, along with Nebojsa, the Russian boy who hardly spoke English but always said hello to me. That was enough for me to consider him a close buddy.

Still, each day something unexpected and unpleasant came my way. On one occasion, while walking on the sidewalk, a car full of older teenagers slowed down and hurled a paper cup of liquid at me. Maybe it was just water but it caught me by surprise, and I jumped.

"Hey Nigger!" they yelled, as they sped off.

That was another word I didn't know the meaning of, but I knew it was intended to hurt. And it did. I also knew it had to do with how I looked.

From that day on, I kept my head down and continued counting the days when I could go back home. I missed the life I had in Iraq, and I wanted to go back to where I belonged.

2

FROM DIPLOMACY TO PIZZA

The Arab League's office was located in Dupont Circle. It was a three-man operation with my father in the lead. His assistant, a young Egyptian man who spoke little English, spent all day cutting and pasting articles (literally, using scissors and glue) about the Middle East from various newspapers like the *Washington Post* and the *New York Times*. From the look of it, the biggest decision they had to make each day was what to have for lunch. A year later, when the Six-Day War between Israel and its surrounding Arab states broke out, everyone in the office was caught with their pants down. They panicked and rather than ramp up their efforts they dimmed the lights and shut down the operation. Shortly thereafter, my father was asked to return to Iraq.

When friends and relatives back home found out that he was planning to come back, they quickly advised him to stay put. "Don't even think about coming back now. It's a mess here," one of my uncles told him. He was referring to the internal political turmoil and the risk of being caught up in it. My father didn't need much convincing. America was the biggest prize. Few people came to America and returned voluntarily. The only hurdle to staying from my father's perspective was finding a job. He needed a way to make a living and raise a family. Everything had to happen quickly. He had to notify his bosses back at the

Arab League that he wasn't coming back. He also had to find a way to obtain legal status now that he was no longer a diplomat.

Within a month, my father would become the unlikeliest owner of a restaurant. Actually, a pizza place in a strip mall in the middle of Annandale, Virginia, thousands of miles away from Baghdad.

The idea of owning a restaurant came up when an Iraqi friend convinced my father that it was a good way to make a decent living in America. The friend had immigrated to the U.S. years earlier and opened a pizza shop near our home. He was older than my father and was suffering from serious health issues. He needed to sell and retire. The place was called Pizza Kaezano. We had eaten there a few times and loved the pizza and steak and cheese subs. On a couple of occasions my father had walked behind the counter and was given a VIP tour. On at least one of those visits he was handed a spatula to make his own custom-made sandwich of pastrami with mustard and onions, his favorite.

"It doesn't take much," the friend assured my father. "The place runs itself. I'll teach you everything you need to know." he told him, adding, "besides, you'll never go hungry. All the food for you and your family, zero dollars." As a family, we rarely went out to eat, and my father never saw himself serving others. Certainly not in a restaurant, wearing an apron. A stoic, serious man, by then in his early forties, he commanded the room and hardly ever laughed. He generally had little time for small talk. Back in Iraq he taught Arabic Literature at Baghdad University.

Up to that moment, it had never crossed my father's mind that running a restaurant was something he would or could do. Weeks earlier he had received an offer from Utah State University to teach Arabic Literature in their newly established Middle Eastern Studies Department. It meant moving the family to Salt Lake City. Being the only job offer on the table at the time, my father accepted it. So when the whole restaurant idea fell into his lap, we were fully packed and ready to make the trip to Utah. By then, my parents had sold many of the Iraqi knick-knacks they had brought with them from Baghdad. Silver urns, Kurdish kilim carpets, hammered copper trays, vases with black onyx etchings and a few hashemiahs, the traditional women's hand-embroidered sheer abayas worn over clothing that my mother had brought with her from Iraq to give away as gifts. They needed the extra cash to supplement the meager salary he was going to make as a part-time professor at Utah State. They held an open house and a crowd descended like vultures on roadkill, departing with valuable Iraqi handmade collectibles acquired for knockdown prices. Decades later, at age 90, my mother still brings up the time she sold this or that "for nothing." "I was so stupid and naive," she laments.

There was no great enthusiasm on my parents' part to move us all across the country, but they didn't have an alternative plan. So when the restaurant idea came up my father regarded it as kismet. How hard could running a pizzeria be? After all, the place was already running and came fully equipped with a solid customer base, a pizza oven, a grill, a fryer, a cash register that never stopped ringing and stable staff that had been there for years. My father, not a man known for taking risks, uncharacteristically emptied his savings account of $50,000 and bought the place. An all-cash deal. No debt. My father didn't believe in debt.

On the day of the purchase, we all piled into our still-new, butter-yellow Impala to check out the joint. It was less than a mile away from home and my school was within walking distance. Located in a suburban strip mall, the storefront was abutted by a movie theater on one side and a pawn shop on the other.

The front door had the hours of business listed in worn gold lettering. Some of the numbers had been scraped off and were written back in with a marker. Taped on the window next to the entrance was a hand-lettered sign that said: "No Shirt, No Shoes, No Come In."

We were greeted on entry by the smell of grilled onions and the sound of a clanging metal spatula against the flat grill. Red and white plastic checkered tablecloths covered the dozen or so tables, and the red velvet fleur-de-lis wallpaper added to the "joint" appeal. A life-size airbrushed tapestry of Elvis Presley with a $10 "for sale" tag hung on one wall. At the other end, a bright neon-lit jukebox pumped out the latest hits from The Ike and Tina Turner Review, Creedence Clearwater Revival and Johnny Cash. The counter, served by a half dozen vinyl swivel stools, was a slightly warped orange Formica with aluminum trim. Two dozen customers took up a few tables, eating, or drinking a beer, some looking at a menu, some waiting for take-out.

My brother, my sister and I quickly slid into one of the olive-green vinyl booths. My father, followed by my mother, walked behind the counter kicking the tires of their new business. They were both dressed to impress. My father wore one of his fancier suits and silk ties. And my mother pulled out all the stops, with one of her signature matching purse-and-shoes combos, complemented with color-coordinated bling. The mostly Arab staff stood by, respectfully looking over their new bosses and welcoming them with various shades of brown-nosing. Meanwhile, the Royal cash register sitting at the edge of the counter, cha-chinged non-stop, a ringing endorsement of the previous owner's "cash cow" sales pitch.

While our parents were getting the VIP tour, my siblings and I were delivered a basket full of crinkle-cut fries and Cokes.

We were ecstatic. I was thirteen at the time, and for the next few years, this place became the center of my universe.

From that day on we became a "restaurant family" with nearly every aspect of our life centered around the joint. Weekends and holidays were no longer occasions to kick back and relax but times to work harder. We closed only for Thanksgiving and Christmas. Those were the rare moments when we became a real family, preparing dinner, watching football, and eating and arguing together without the threat of someone calling about an unexpected disaster at the restaurant.

The place not only reeked of onion, it also reeked of white America. In the entire time we were there hardly a person of color came through those doors. I was still self-conscious of the way I looked and tried to blend in. In short order it became my "America" boot camp, the place where I honed my American slang, learned to code switch by assuming a new half-Italian identity to match the menu. The other half changed with whomever I was serving at the time. French, Swiss, Greek. Being Arab was not something to be proud of in 1967 America.

Pizza Kaezano was your typical neighborhood crossroad greasy spoon, where lawyers and doctors drank beer and shot the breeze alongside construction workers and mail carriers. Where everyone knew everyone. It was a place where you found a plumber if you needed one or got a recommendation for a local dentist. It was Cheers before there was Cheers and I was working my way up to be Sam Malone.

It was also here that I learned the secret art of making pizza—adding root beer to the dough to make it crispier. How to make a killer meatball using Parmesan cheese, lots of dry

basil and soaking stale bread in milk. I discovered I loved cooking and in time learned about how to use spices and herbs to
refine a sauce. Too much oregano, for instance, can make a
sauce bitter. Adding Worcestershire sauce to meat sauce gives it
a kick and a meatier taste. Frying potatoes twice by blanching
them first makes them crispier. I also learned that salt is the
most underrated seasoning and can make or break a dish. The
deadliest word for a restaurant is bland. These lessons would
come in handy later in my restaurant career.

It was also there that I became Andy. It happened uncere-
moniously. The name was given to me by a regular customer
named Bob, the neighborhood alcoholic. He had a scruffy
white beard and untamed hair. He looked like he had just come
out of a fight. One day, while sitting at the counter, I brought
him a draft beer and emptied his overflowing ashtray. "You're a
gentleman and scholar," he said, flashing more gum than teeth.
"What's your name?" he asked. "Anas," I responded. "What?"
he said, in his gravelly voice. I repeated my name. He made several failed attempts at pronouncing it. Finally, he gave up. "I'll
just call you Andy. How's that? You look like an Andy," he said,
bursting into a coughing fit.

The name stuck with me after that day. It was one less obstacle I had to deal with and made interactions with customers
a lot smoother. People stopped asking me where I was from.
But I felt like an imposter, someone who was trying to pass, to
blend.

The claim by the previous owner about the "place running
itself" was largely true. The manager of the restaurant, Ghazi,
a twenty-year-old Palestinian workhorse with a penchant for
blond teenyboppers, put in an 80-hour, six-days-per-week
schedule. On the days Ghazi worked, my father only needed to
do spot visits to empty the register, which had a steady stream
of cash throughout the day and to make sure that Ghazi was

not too distracted by his numerous love interests, whom he won over with an occasional free order of fries and a soda.

Sundays, however, were a different story. This was Ghazi's day off, which I am certain he spent sleeping. For my father it was the worst day of the week because he then had to run the restaurant himself. We'd watch his blood pressure rise as the week progressed, and then when Sundays came my brother, my sister and I would accompany him to the restaurant early in the morning. We had no choice. Once inside, we were met with the stale smell of overnight grease and beer that quickly evaporated once the hood fan was turned on and the grill and pizza oven were fired up. We would spread out like an army platoon with an attack plan. I was in charge of setting up the salad line, my brother, the pizza line and my sister, who was only nine at the time, would make sure that the tables were wiped and the sugar and salt and pepper shakers were full. My father gave her a quarter or two to play music on the jukebox, and then would count the bills and coins in the register to make sure that there was enough change to start the day. He helped out a bit in the kitchen, making meatballs and batches of pizza sauce. He took serious pride in his meatballs, which he thought were amazing. He never used a recipe, just two handfuls of this, one handful of that, and lots of oregano. He loved oregano and put it in everything. It was his signature flavor. Sometimes he would even use oregano to disguise the flavor of meat that was questionable.

But with the exception of preparing the meatballs and collecting the cash, my father did not relish his role as a pizza shop owner. This was not what he imagined life in America to be. As a diplomat, he was used to being pampered and now the tables had been turned. My father also had a short temper, which got in the way of managing staff or dealing with difficult customers.

One Sunday morning, a man came in soon after my father unlocked the door. He ordered two large pizzas. My father made the pizzas while the customer waited in a booth nursing a bottle of Schlitz. Once the pizzas came out of the oven, my father let him know that they were ready and placed them next to the counter. When the man did not respond, my father ignored him and went about his opening routine assuming that the man wanted to continue drinking his beer.

Sometime later, the man yelled from the booth in a tone that made the hairs on my father's back bristle, "Hey man, how much longer for them pies?"

My father responded curtly with his broken, heavy-accented English, "They are ready here for long time."

Visibly annoyed, the man got up, swaggered over to the counter and placed his hand on the pizza box. "Hey man, these are cold. I ain't payin' for no cold pies. You gotta make me new ones, old man."

My father stared at the guy for a moment with a furrowed brow. I could see the temperature rising in his head, his temper flaring. After an exchange of tangled words that quickly escalated into shouting, he turned silent, recoiling like a cobra ready to strike, and then, with one quick swoop, his hands shaking, he picked up the two boxes and hurled them squarely at the man's chest. The pizzas flew out, covering the man with dripping red sauce and cheese. "Get out, stupid man!" My father yelled, "get out!" The man ran out of the restaurant shouting back, "You fuckin' crazy sand nigger."

Luckily there were no other customers in the place. I stood watching the spectacle unfold, stuck somewhere between shock and disbelief having just received a lesson in "Customer Service 101: What Not To Do!" Then I quickly brought out rags and a mop to clean up the mess. My father didn't say a word and went about setting up for the day. By midday, he and my sister would go home, leaving me and my brother to run the show.

As the weeks went by my brother and I learned to accept our fate as de facto slave labor. Business boomed and over time my father's attitude toward the restaurant changed. He became much more convivial, making small talk with the regulars at the counter anytime he came in for his regular drive-by empty-the-register-and-run routines. Everyone called him Doc, a title he relished because it reminded those around him that he was more than just a pizza man. Occasionally he would make a batch of meatballs or his usual pastrami sub with onion and mustard, but for the most part he left day-to-day operations to Ghazi and his sons.

This arrangement suited my brother and me just fine. The restaurant was a hangout for our school friends, which gave us a much-needed boost in popularity. With a free order of fries or a soda, you can pretty much win over anyone. Over time, I learned to love the business and became adept at dealing with people from every walk of life. Mostly I just listened, smiled and nodded my head. My English was still not great, and I had a stutter.

I felt joy serving the regulars and looked forward to seeing them on Sundays. Even at 13, I was in my element. I kept imagining what I would do if the joint was mine. I mean really mine. What would I do differently? I never let on to my father that I actually loved serving. I knew it would disappoint him. To him, serving was something done for him, not by him. The restaurant business was a temporary way to make a living and put us through school. He saw little future in it for either my brother or me. He wish was for me to be a doctor and my brother an engineer. He got half of what he hoped for.

Nevertheless, the pizza shop gave my father independence and a decent living. There was no one to answer to. No boss. My father didn't do well with bosses. In his eyes, the restaurant business, although lucrative enough to support his family, lacked prestige. It also required having to deal face-to-face with people with whom he had little in common and generally didn't much like. The drunk at the bar. The hard-to-please customer who made demands and who looked down on him. Employees and all the baggage that came with them. It wore him out. Any incident, whether small or large, could send him over the edge. If a customer was being a little difficult, they were asked to leave and to never come back. If an employee asked for a raise regarded as unreasonable, they would be fired within days. And good luck collecting that final paycheck. My father was the original Soup Nazi from "Seinfeld."

Despite all that, the restaurant delivered what was promised. During the first year, my parents were able to purchase a nice home with a swimming pool, albeit above ground, put us through college and stash away some savings.

When my brother and I started college, my father couldn't run the place on his own. Within weeks he found himself forced into making a deal with Ghazi. They agreed on a partnership in which Ghazi would pay my father a fixed monthly amount. Nothing formal was signed. It was a handshake deal that put my father in the driver seat, allowing him to pull the rug out at a moment's notice. Ghazi went from working six days a week to moving into the place, literally. He built a loft above the kitchen with a bed, so that he could take naps during afternoon lulls in the business. The bed was also well-used after hours. The title of owner gave Ghazi clout and elevated his stock with the local posse of women. It also gave my father the freedom to look for other opportunities. It was what he believed to be a win-win, where he did most of the winning.

3

BUSBOYS BOOT CAMP

The first job that I got paid for outside of my father's place was at a small sandwich shop called Lums. It was during the summer before college, I was 15 and by then I had a good amount of training working at Pizza Kaezano. Lums was a brightly-lit sliver of a diner on Georgia Avenue smack dab in the middle of Silver Spring, Maryland, that served transient truckers as well as locals. It was open well after midnight serving footlong hotdogs with sauerkraut and stacked Reuben sandwiches that required both hands to eat. They came slathered with Thousand Island dressing and mounds of coleslaw on the side. Most of the place was taken up by a long stainless steel counter with a row of well-used stools leaving room for about a dozen booths and tables. At the end of the counter sat a large jar with whole dill pickles that Lums was known for. They were more salty than sour, the way I like them, and retained their crunch for days. For most of that summer, I worked the late night shift, which meant arriving at three in the afternoon and not leaving till around three the following morning.

The day I got the job, I was so excited, I didn't bother to ask what hours I'd be working or what exactly I'd be doing. Hell, I didn't even know how much I was getting paid. All I knew was that I was going to make money. Money to me meant independence. With money, I could do what I wanted and say what

I wanted. I wouldn't have to answer to my parents. I knew I had to start somewhere and Lums was as good a place as any.

Lums was a boot camp. My manager there was an ex-Marine. Or, as he would say, "Once a Marine always a Marine." He was close to six and a half feet tall, barrel-chested and had one eye missing leaving a dull gray half-closed socket in its place in need of a patch. A drool-filled unlit cigar stub that he chomped on incessantly dangled from his mouth. He resembled the bad guy in Popeye, only meaner. He had a smart-ass line for everything and a nickname for each of his minions.

I was soon christened "Handy Andy" and my goal was never to give him a reason to pick on me or give me a less flattering title. If he liked you, you were spared the abuse that came with the job, if he didn't; then he became the Manager From Hell. It was his way or the highway.

One morning the Manager From Hell noticed that the floor had not been mopped well from the night before. He was fuming and waited until the rest of the crew arrived. He pulled everyone in a huddle and, slowly one-eyeing everyone, announced deliberately, "Whoever mopped the floor should mop it one more time and then do us all a favor and shoot themselves." It sounded like he meant it. He then proceeded to give us a lesson in floor mopping 101 that I have yet to forget. "Figure of eight, just like that, figure of eight," he kept repeating while sloshing the wet mop from side to side in a circular motion. "None of this sissy back-and-forth shit. All you're doing is pushing all the goddam dirt to the corners. You ain't supposed to fuck the goddam floor with this back and forth shit, you're supposed to mop it. Now here, you try it," he abruptly handed the mop to Chunky Chuck, the person whom he suspected was the culprit, and who by that point was sweating like a thief in a lineup. "See how easy that is?" he said, watching CC quickly doing figures of eight. When he was satisfied that he had thoroughly humiliated him, he walked away chomping on his wet cigar and muttering a few choice swear words under his breath. That's when he ran into Lazy Susie: "What the hell are you standing there for? Get back to work," he said, "if you can lean, you can clean." I took the job seriously and tried to outdo everyone with my advanced figures of eight and never standing around without a rag in one hand at the ready.

Despite Manager From Hell, I liked the work at Lums. I loved cooking and I loved the rare praise that came from MFH. By the time I left, I had earned the unofficial title of Kiss-Ass Andy. I didn't care, knowing that it was my hard work that earned me a quarter raise within the first six weeks. By the end of the summer, I was making the dazzling sum of $2.25 per hour.

Back at home, it was a different story. My parents hated the fact that I worked so late. They hated that their son cooked and cleaned and mopped floors for other people. And they wondered where they went wrong. Even though they owned a restaurant, for them it was just a way to make it in America. They had no other choice. It was not a career, not for them and certainly not for their children. They wanted better for us. A job that required a suit and tie. A desk. Maybe a secretary.

On more than one occasion, they threatened to disown me, but I was defiant and kept at it. I was a teenage stew of hormonal angst, inviting strangers into the house, staying out till dawn and generally being fingernails on a chalkboard for my parents. They took away my car privileges, which meant that the trip back and forth to work became a real journey. The closest bus stop was nearly a mile away and I had to be there at least 30 minutes early to make sure I didn't miss the one bus that got me there on time. The way back was even more challenging. The buses stopped running at midnight and I was stuck either walking or hitchhiking the four miles home. At 3 or 4 in the morning only strange people are picking up hitchhikers and I attracted enough of them. There was the one guy who put his hands on my knee and told me how much he would like to "clean my pipes" and his affinity for "dark meat." I had him let me off several blocks away from my house and made sure he was way out of sight before I unclenched my fists and walked home. Another time someone was so drunk that he asked me to drive while he passed out in the passenger seat. I drove myself home, turned off the ignition and left him sleeping in the car, two blocks away from my home. Looking back at the Lums summer, it's a miracle that I wasn't found drugged and dismembered in some creep's basement.

The next summer, I got a job at Leonie's, a bustling Italian restaurant with checkered tablecloths, dripping colored candles over Chianti bottles and surly waiters who told you what to order and didn't take no for an answer. The place was dark and velvety and oozing with the smell of garlic. They kept the lights low to hide the stains on the mostly red wall-to-wall carpet. It matched the color of most of the entrees. Classic Italian dishes like lasagna, manicotti and spaghetti with fancy sauces like bolognese, marinara and alfredo.

I loved waiting tables, and the money wasn't bad either. Most of the waiters and waitresses at Leonie's were old-school. Efficient. No frills. For them, it was about the money. How to get the most by doing the least. They had little patience for customers who lingered, ones who couldn't make up their mind and those who requested lots of modification or asked for everything on the side. The ROI on those customers didn't add up. They would hustle them through, drop the check and hover over the table removing every utensil, glasses, salt and pepper shakers down to the bare tablecloth if they lingered too long.

Once in a while they would ask them to leave point-blank, causing a ruckus and a manager to intervene. At Leonie's the customer wasn't always right. The veteran waiters ran the show. I, on the other hand, did no such thing. I did not rush my customers and continued to refill their water until the very end. Nor did I try to upsell the most expensive special or trick the customer into buying the priciest bottle of wine just to earn a larger tip. I was genuinely interested in serving them. To the other waiters, I was trouble. A spike in their cranky wheel. They had "trained the customers" over the years to a certain style and anyone messing with that was bound to be a pain in the butt.

"Be careful when you meet a very nice customer. They'll tip you with their smile and nice words. No thank you! You can have the nice ones," an old timer told me during my two -hour orientation training. It was more of an initiation than a training. He'd been there for decades and was more than a little jaded. "I prefer the professional diners. They come, they eat, they drink, they spend money, they tip and they leave. They know how to tip," he said.

Each customer was assessed way before being seated. White businessmen were ranked at the top, followed by white couples on a date and so on. At the bottom were Black people, brown people, foreigners and families with small children. "Those people will run you to death and leave loose change," I was warned.

Leonie's was a racism boot camp. The waiters argued in the back about being stiffed or getting the "Black ones" and making racist jokes about anyone and everyone: Blacks, Arabs, Jews, you name it. No one was off limits, and no one was worse than the Black customers, "who not only stiffed you but worked you to the bone." One of them turned to me, after a tirade over a bad tip, and said, "Tell your people to learn how to tip." He either mistook me for Black or lumped any non-white person in the same category. He was referring to the Black party he just waited on. I was surprised they left him any tip at all. He stank of disdain and contempt. And even though he thought he was hiding it under the guise of "professionalism," they could surely smell his racism a mile away, like a cheap cologne.

No one wanted the Black parties and the hostesses knew it. They would make sure that those folks were seated in the newest or least experienced waiters' sections. The other servers would threaten the hostess with physical harm or sometimes pay them a bribe to make sure they got the cream of the crop, the white businessmen. The snowflakes, as they were called. This usually meant that I got most of the "leftovers," the Black parties and those with small children. My section looked like the back of a Montgomery, Alabama, bus. I was determined to prove them wrong, after all I was an Arab, a foreigner to boot, and was often seen as Black. In many instances Black customers became my best tippers.

People tip well when served with grace and dignity and when you treat them like you would want to be treated. Being nice actually pays off most of the time. Whenever I received a less-than-generous tip, rather than blame it on the guest, I would think of ways that I could have done better. I made sure to anticipate the guest's needs before they asked. I learned that the best way to get families with small children to tip well is to be nice to their children. "Let me get you some crackers for the baby," I would say. By the time the summer was over, I had developed my own non-hustle. I was the "nice" one and was walking out with as much in tips as the vets, and frequently more. My coworkers would make jokes about how I was able to "milk" each table. "What do you do? Do you give your customers hand jobs?" one waiter quipped.

The chef at Leonie's, Mr. Lee, was a piece of work. He was a husky Asian man who wore a black bandana headband with

Japanese lettering on it and spoke in a heavily accented English that required some getting used to. He had been at Leonie's for ages and had little patience for whiny customers. There would be hell to pay when a new waiter came into the kitchen to tell him that someone didn't like something. The older ones knew better. They would just deal with it and sometimes even pay for the food themselves to avoid his wrath. It was too risky to tell Mr. Lee, who might retort, "Tell dos fagots to stop sucking so much of dick. Maybe den day can taste da food."

He had a deep dislike for waiters and thought that most were lazy and spoiled. They had the easy jobs, he thought. They just showed up and raked in the cash. No sweat. No heat. No elbows deep in grease at the end of the night. He would berate any waiter who was not on their top game and frequently chased them out of "his" kitchen with a butcher knife if they were loafing around or picking off a French fry or a piece of lettuce from someone's plate. This was one of his pet peeves and God help you if he saw you touching or even thinking about touching the food with your "filty fingas." He chose his victims carefully and once in a while he would heat up a plate under the salamander and place it on the pickup line just in time for an unsuspecting newly hired waiter to reach for it. "Pick up," he would yell. You would hear the scream in the dining room followed by cursing and a cascade of broken dishes. Mr. Lee would stand there in triumph half grinning through the pickup line knowing that his point was made and that the distance between the back of the house and the front of the house was maintained for another cohort of servers.

By the end of the summer, I was ready to go. I'd had enough of Mr. Lee and his antics and didn't get along with most of the waiters either. They were a bitter lot of old hags and curmudgeons. Somewhere along the way they had lost their joy of service, and I never wanted to see myself becoming one of them.

4

DROPPING OUT

My parents were the opposite of helicopter parents. In their mind, they did you a favor by bringing you into this world and it was on you to make the best of it. In Iraq, the village helps to raise the child. But now, the village they once knew and trusted was gone. So, they did what most parents would do in their situation: They became quasi-prison wardens. Hours outside the home were heavily restricted. Friends were forbidden from coming inside the house. Anyone who was not Arab was not allowed past our front door. And even then, they had to be vetted. They trusted no one. We were under 24-hour surveillance.

All through my teens my world was limited to school, the pizza place and television. I spoke very little English and the few words I knew sounded like dictionary English and often solicited laughter. To make things even worse, I stuttered. For the most part, for the first few years of being in America, I kept to myself, smiled a lot and spoke only when absolutely necessary.

Having skipped two grades, I was able to catch up with my older brother to graduate from high school the same year as he did. In my family, graduating from high school was not considered an accomplishment. It was expected. A PhD or another professional degree, maybe, but not high school. Celebrating a high school graduation to my parents lowered expectations and sent the wrong signal. In fact, neither my parents nor my brother and I bothered to attend the ceremony, opting to receive our diplomas by mail. I never bothered to look at mine. To make things even less inconvenient for my parents, both my brother and I applied to the same university, thus making our commute easier.

Catholic University was about a half-hour away from our home. It was the college of choice for my parents. Back in Baghdad, the best schools were run by Jesuits and even though CU was not a Jesuit school, it was close enough for them. They were known for their rigorous academics and strict moral standards. On the first day of school, my brother and I had an early morning class. It was a relatively chilly day and I was all nerves. I had just turned 15 and the idea of college was scary as hell. I had no idea what to expect and the last thing I wanted was for anyone to know how old I was. We stopped at the 7-Eleven on the way to buy a pack of cigarettes. I smoked Tareytons, my brother, Marlboros. I had picked up smoking that year to appear older, readying myself for college.

We arrived at school early and sat in the car puffing away, going over our class schedules and deciding on a rendezvous time. We headed out to our respective classes and didn't see each other until the end of the day when we met at the car to head home. We relied on notes left on the windshield to communicate with one another. On days when my brother had a late class or a soccer practice or was just plain MIA, I would spend the time either in the library or at my favorite spot, The National Shrine cafeteria. There I would waste away the hours drinking free coffee refills, averaging about 8-10 cups per visit.

One day my brother was later than usual. He was nowhere to be found. The only clue that I had was that he was dating a girl who lived in a nearby dorm. The building was centrally located and I had met her roommate, Chris, once. When I knocked on the door, Chris answered and invited me in. The room was tiny. Enough for two twin-sized beds and two desks. A large poster of Jane Fonda as Barbarella with "Who can save the world?" written at the top hung on one wall. One of the beds was left unmade with clothing spread across it. "I just did laundry," Chris said apologetically. "That's okay," I responded.

I sat on the edge of her bed. We talked non-stop while Chris put the pile of clothing in a hamper and continued to tidy up the room, moving books around and rearranging pillows. My brother and his girlfriend, Alicia, finally showed up two hours later.

My visits to the dorm became a regular thing; sometimes I would be hanging out with Chris well into the night. Over time, Chris and I became good friends. We even started dating and later married. I was 20 when we got married and predictably, the marriage lasted a handful of years. Throughout our courtship, I had to lie about my age, adding three years. I did that for most of the time I was in college. It was the only way to get a date or a beer at the Rathskeller. When she found out that she was four years older than me, she was mortified and almost called off the wedding. Things went downhill from there.

Chris was a Speech Pathology and Audiology major. One afternoon she mentioned that she noticed that I stuttered. She said it so matter-of-factly it took me by surprise. I was stunned and turned every shade of purple. She added that there was a stutterers support group that met weekly on campus.

"I think you will like them. They are a great group of people," she said assuredly. Until then, I had thought that I was hiding my stuttering pretty well. I never imagined getting therapy for my speech or saw myself as a "stutterer" per se. I had hoped that in time, the problem would take care of itself. Nonetheless, I wanted to play along.

I arrived early for the first meeting. My heart raced as I walked up the cobblestone steps leading into the building that housed the speech and audiology program. Inside, there were a couple of men deep in conversation. One stood out. He was impeccably dressed and had a well-trimmed graying beard. He quickly approached me. "Hi, Mmy nnnnaaame isss BBBBrad," he said. "Nice to mmeeeet you. Mmy name isss AAAndy," I said, slightly stuttering. His gaze never left mine. "PPPllleease gggrab a ssseeeaat," he said. He was a professional stage actor who performed Shakespeare for a living. He stuttered while speaking to me in a way that I had never seen anyone do before. His stuttering seemed natural, and strangely effortless. He kept eye contact the entire time while speaking to me. I was surprised that he was able to be an actor with such an obvious speech impediment. Within minutes after sitting down, I was surrounded by about twenty mostly middle-aged men and a handful of women. At 15, I was by far the youngest.

Brad's stuttering vanished when he assumed his character's role onstage. This is true for most stutterers. We can hide our stutter behind a persona that we create, sometimes slightly changing an accent or intonation throughout a conversation. For most non-stutterers this is difficult to understand; to me it made perfect sense. I had used the same trick many times to get through a conversation. Over the years, since then, I tried every kind of therapy for my speech. None of them seemed to work. Once, a therapist suggested that I stick a pencil in my mouth, from cheek to cheek like a horse bit, and speak like that for an hour every day. His theory was that once I removed the pencil, regular speech would feel much easier. Other therapists made me roll on the floor, do breathing exercises, and slow down my speech. Most of them were quacks. Nonetheless I was determined to overcome this obstacle. I continued to attend weekly meetings and got referrals to all kinds of speech therapists. I was just about ready to throw in the towel, having tried every trick in the book. It wasn't until I was well into my thirties when I met the person who would hand me the key to fluency.

Vivian was a rising star in the stuttering therapy field. She had recently opened a practice in downtown DC. Her approach to stuttering therapy shattered all myths and went to the root of the issue. Stuttering, she theorized, is not a speech disorder but rather a mental issue. In other words, stuttering is in your head, not in your tongue. Her theory confirmed what I intuitively knew. When I arrived for my first appointment, she welcomed me and made sure I understood this wasn't a silver bullet. It was hard work and required commitment.

She called it "fear reduction" therapy. If the fear of stuttering could be removed, she believed the stuttering would eventually be reduced and possibly eliminated altogether. Of course, to remove the fear, you had to face it. I would have to feel comfortable stuttering without fear of judgment and ridicule. I would have to let go of my inhibitions and the trauma of past experiences and "out" myself as a stutterer.

"Are you in?" She asked with a smile.

I smiled back and nodded my head.

For my first therapy session, Vivian placed a phone in front of me and asked me to dial 411. When the operator answered, she told me to ask for a name and a phone number, it could be of anyone. "Here is the trick," she said. "I want you to stutter the entire time. Don't try to work around words, or substitute words that feel less scary, just stutter with abandon. It's that easy and that hard," she added. I went ahead and dialed 411 and once the operator answered, I stuttered and stuttered and stuttered some more. It took nearly 10 minutes to ask a simple question. The stuttering came out like a gushing waterfall. As if a dam had broken. When the call ended, sweat was beading on my forehead and I was nearly out of breath.

"How did that feel?" Vivian asked. "It felt great," I replied, taking a big exhale. Being able to stutter without fear or judgment was an incredible feeling that I had never experienced before. For the first time in my life I did not feel ashamed of stuttering.

"This is the easy part. Now you have to go into the world out there," Vivian said, pointing toward the window, "and stutter in front of friends and people who know you. That's the hard part."

That day, I walked away, having been handed a key to a door that I had been trying to open ever since I was a child.

Years later, I ran into Vivian and thanked her for changing my life. She was the director of the Center for Speech Pathology and Audiology at The University of Maryland. She was so excited to see me and was happy that things had worked out well for me. A few days later she called me and invited me to be the commencement speaker at the school.

After finishing college I had little idea what to do next. I had majored in biology and the plan was to go straight to medical school. This was my parents' plan, not mine. To me, the idea of becoming a doctor seemed far-fetched. I fainted at the sight of blood. I had little patience when it came to caring for the sick. And I was pretty sure I wasn't studious enough to make the commitment required to pass medical exams. I was just 19 and I felt I needed a break from education.

Nevertheless, I applied to Howard University Medical School and after one semester I realized I was in over my head. But where could I go from there? With a degree in biology my options were limited. I started a job as a medical immunology technician at the National Cancer Institute. I spent most of my day staring into a microscope at slides or identifying growth patterns on Petri dishes and filling out clipboards. After a couple of months the work proved to be mind-numbingly repetitive. Less than a year in, I decided to call it quits and ditch my medical studies altogether. I had stopped looking forward to going to work; the days were dragging on and on. I had to figure out a way to pay for rent by doing something new. Something completely different.

5

TRICKS OF THE TRADE

The day I left the NIH, I had just $1,000 in the bank. It barely covered one month of rent. I grabbed the paper and started scouring the want ads, circling a few restaurants that were hiring. I needed some fast income to tide me over until I could figure out what to do with my life. Being a server was a good temporary option. This time, I decided to apply at the fancier places, where the pay was higher and the clientele more sophisticated. When I got a call back from a place called 209 1/2 I was ecstatic. 209 1/2 was an upscale, 40-seat boutique restaurant that had garnered lots of dining awards and frequently made the *Washington Post* Best Restaurants list. It was located just a stone's throw away from the US Capitol and catered to Hill staffers and their bosses, senators, congressmen and the men and women who buttered their bread, the lobbyists. The food was nouvelle cuisine, which, in the early '80s, had become the hottest fad in upscale dining. It featured large fancy plates with small portions, decorated with a smear of this and a sprig of that, servings that left you craving a Big Mac on the way home.

I loved working at 209 1/2. It was a far more cultured scene than Lum's or Leonie's and for the first time I felt like a professional. The waiters were called "waitrons," and everyone worked well together and pooled tips. In time, they became my closest friends. If you didn't get along with everyone and didn't pull your weight, you were quickly shown the way out. There was no room for slackers and far less backstabbing and petty gossip. Each person was part of the team and did everything from hosting to bartending to tending to the flowers. It felt like being part of a family and we'd often all go out together for drinks after a long day at work.

The customers at 209 1/2 were cultured and worldly and did not hesitate to order the $100 bottles of wine, or the $25 Chesapeake crab cake entree with zucchini fritters. The fritters, a signature dish of the restaurant, were made every day at the bar before lunch. The kitchen was so small that it was necessary to do most of the prep in the dining room before we opened. I would frequently come in early to help out with grating the zucchini or peeling vegetables. All the recipes for the dishes were top secret, especially the fritters. From what I could tell, they were made with equal amounts of grated zucchini and potatoes, a few eggs and salt and pepper mixed together and left to chill in the refrigerator, then formed into palm size patties and fried to a brown crisp in a pan of shallow oil. They came with most of the entrees and people would frequently order a few extras on the side. I tried making them at home but they were never the same as the ones at 209 1/2. I suspect the secret was the addition of a pinch of baking soda. Frequently something simple like that makes all the difference.

Daniel, the manager, was a flamboyant gay guy, chubby with a receding hairline. He admired my work ethic and willingness to jump in wherever I was needed; changing the water for the flowers or even cleaning the bathrooms when necessary. I was a multitasker, having learned this essential restaurant trait back in the days of Pizza Kaezano. He took me under his wing. He soon made it clear that it wasn't just my can-do attitude to work that he appreciated. "I like my men like my coffee, strong and black," he told me one day, quoting a line from Lauren Bacall, and added, "I like it even better with a little cream." When he found out I was Arab, he said half-jokingly with his arms flailing, "That's even better, I'm Jewish. We can make peace in the Middle East!" Though I couldn't fulfil his wishes, I kept alive his hopes for the sake of job security.

Within six weeks of starting at 209 1/2 I became Daniel's unofficial assistant. He would pay me a few extra bucks to act as head waiter, opening or closing the restaurant when needed. "You're too good to be just a waitron, Andy," he told me. Too good seemed to me a strange way to put it. Serving is one of those things you're either good at or you're not. Later I learned that you cannot train someone to want to serve. Sure, you can go over the technical aspects of serving but it is the desire to please others that is the key ingredient of good service. Not everyone has that in them.

The opportunity to work alongside Daniel and learn the ins and outs of the business was too good to pass up. Despite his flirtations, he was great fun to be with and, at the same time, the consummate professional, with an encyclopedic knowledge of everything, from the wine to the liquors, to the aperitifs. He had a painstaking focus on detail which bordered on obsessive compulsive disorder.

"The details are what matters, the rest just happens," he would often repeat. Every morning, right before we opened for lunch at 11:30 on the dot, he would have the three waitrons working that day stand at attention with our fingers pointing out for a full inspection. Nails had to be clean, shoes shined, and uniforms pressed. We each had to be equipped with a lighter, wine opener and three pens, black, retractable and of the same brand. It made for a more uniform look when hooked to the short black aprons we wore. "There is a reason why it's called a uniform," he would say. He would even smell our breath.

"Nobody wants to smell smoke or bad breath while eating," he said.

Despite this rigor, being a server at 209 1/2 was the easiest money I had ever made, walking away with two bills for a few hours of work. My step into assisting Daniel felt like a nudge to get into management. A part of me was hesitant to take that on. In the restaurant business, it usually meant making less money and working much longer hours.

In any case, I continued to work harder than ever. I was driven and eager to learn and wanted to be the best at what I did. The owners, Jason Wollen and his mother, Rose, having heard about my rave reviews from the regulars as well as Daniel, were thrilled to know that I was committed to the job. Jason was the head honcho. He wore blindingly white starched button-up shirts over equally white T's outlined by a ring of black chest hair. His shirt was always firmly tucked into perfectly creased belted khakis, emphasizing a slight paunch. He wore black, thick-rimmed glasses that he continually pushed back with his middle finger, and penny loafers complete with a penny tucked inside, always heads up for good luck. Everything about Jason was robotic and slightly awkward. He moved jerkily, like a synchronized swimmer but without the grace. He was the original 40-year-old virgin and lived with Rose in a fancy townhouse in Arlington. I had to deliver something to his home one day and waited in the gold-trimmed foyer with a huge chandelier and an elevator. Beyond the entrance I could see two throne-like chairs in the living room. Thick curtains with golden tassels and enough fabric to cover a football field framed the tall windows. I expected Liberace to waltz in at any minute. It was the first time I had seen an elevator in a private home. Someday, I thought, I could own a house like this (without the Liberace decor).

Jason came into the restaurant once a day, made a few quick observations and left. He would stand in one corner, swivel his neck like an owl and swoop toward a shelf or a corner as if zeroing in on prey. He would run his index finger across the bar or a wall ledge and show it to me or anyone else nearby without saying a word. His eyes and tight lips said it all. He didn't use a white glove, but he might as well have. No matter how hard we tried to clear the dust, he always seemed to find the one spot that was missed. Still, he was generally satisfied that we showed care and initiative and to him that was worth something. He also seemed to take sadistic comfort in the fact that I and the rest of the staff were terrified of him.

His inspections didn't just stop with a finger swab; he also went behind the bar and eyeballed the wine and liquor stock, then stepped into the kitchen with a handful of spoons to taste a soup or a sauce. Occasionally, he would sample a just-cooked zucchini fritter and give instant feedback. Saying nothing meant things were good. I'm aware of at least one occasion when he fired a cook on the spot. Said cook had fried a few fritters and burned them on one side, but rather than chucking them, he flipped them over to hide his mistake. This is the biggest *faux pas* in the restaurant business: knowingly serving a badly cooked dish.

Sometimes Jason would come at night for dinner with his current love interest. He would appear to be fully engrossed in the date yet the next day I would get a full report about the food and the service with every detail vividly critiqued, from the wine service to the check, which was individually hand inscribed for each guest by the bartender, who doubled up as the cashier. His mother Rose had a different demeanor when she played hostess on busy nights. She was loud and brash, with lots of lipstick and big blonde hair teased out with so much hair spray that the staff were nervous when lighting a candle in her vicinity. Her earrings sparkled from a mile away, her pearls made their way around her neck several times, and she wore rings that would likely cause her to lose a finger or a hand in a Jakarta market. She often drank too many Bouvet mimosas throughout the night. "Andy, my glass must have a hole in it. Can you get me another Bou-vet," she would say, cracking up into fits of laughter. I laughed along and complied. By the end of most nights she was teetering on being wasted and when reservations were backed up, she would not hesitate to grab the coats of guests from the coat closet and stand next to their table signaling, in a not-so-subtle way, that it was time for them to leave. I would follow behind her, trying to repair the damage by apologizing profusely, sometimes offering a free drink or dessert. Despite her lack of tact, I learned a lot from Rose. She knew most of the customers by name and remembered details about their children and families. "How's Bobby doing in school?" she would ask. Or she might say, "You're in luck today, the chef has your favorite special. Andy, make sure they hold the coho salmon for Mr. and Mrs. So-and-so. Tell the chef to make it extra special." I enjoyed watching her weave her magic in the dining room.

Perhaps my most memorable encounter with Rose occurred when I first started working at 209 1/2. I was standing at one end of the restaurant when a guest walked in. Not knowing what was expected of me, I just stood there and smiled. Rose, standing next to me, didn't miss a step. She gave me a sturdy push toward the door, with her hand against the small of my back, while whispering loudly: "What are you waiting for? Stop staring at the door and seat the guests!" I almost tripped over myself, more embarrassed than upset. Until today, I can still feel the push of Rose's hand in the center of my back when a guest walks into one of my restaurants. I learned that day that you don't just stand there, you do something, you run toward them, you do anything to make sure they feel noticed.

6

A MOTH TRAPPED IN A JAR

In short order I had become the star server at 209 1/2. Cozying up to every VIP that Rose wanted to impress, I would pull out all the stops to make sure that I remembered their names, their favorite table, and what they ate and drank on their previous visit. I was very good at it. So it was no surprise that Jason called me into his office one afternoon to discuss a management position. Part of me was thrilled at the promotion, another part loved the freedom of less responsibility. I was still trying to figure out what to do with my life.

Jason transferred me to 209 1/2's sister restaurant, the Foggy Bottom Café, a small, stylish place tucked into a residential area under a boutique hotel called the River Inn within walking distance of the Kennedy Center. The Foggy Bottom Café was popular among Kennedy Center theatergoers and the neighbors who lived in this fancy tree-lined part of town. It was ahead of its time, boasting casual elegance with modern recessed lighting, sheer curtains, sleek wooden tables and chairs and a marble-tiled floor. The menu was equally minimalist, featuring a handful of dishes like scrod with caper hollandaise, vegetable tempura, peanut noodles with ginger and a filet mignon with a demi-glace and shiitake mushrooms. The food was efficient, simple and well-prepared.

Christopher, the general manager, was not enthused about training me. Having heard Daniel sing my praises, he saw me as a threat. He was being transferred to a new place that the Wollens were about to open on Connecticut Avenue. Another themed restaurant, this one named after Mrs. Wallis Simpson, the famous Baltimore divorcée who scandalously married King Edward VIII, causing him to abdicate the throne. I had heard that Christopher wasn't thrilled about moving.

On my first day of training, I stood next to Christopher at one corner of the small dining room, observing the servers weaving through the narrow spaces between the tables while he pointed out every tiny detail of service. Like Jason and Daniel, Christopher was a stickler for small things. His mantra echoed theirs: if you take care of the details, the other stuff will take care of itself. He took this to lengths that verged on the absurd, pointing out the tiniest things like servers that did not have their hands behind their back when speaking to a table, or someone who did not greet the table within the targeted 30 seconds, or base plates that were left on the table when the server walked away after taking the food order. "People don't go out to eat, they go out to dine," he observed, and dining was all about the details. He wanted to impress me with his knowledge, which I had to admit was admirable.

Once Christoper departed for his new post, the next few days of training were spent in the kitchen with Jacqui, a Jamaican chef with whom I hit it off right away. She was an undocumented immigrant who had come to the U.S. on a student visa and, while working part-time in kitchens to support herself, had discovered her love for cooking. In due course she left school and worked her way up the chain to become a chef. In those days, being a female chef was nearly unheard of. Being a Black female chef was as rare as a rainy day in a Baghdad summer.

I was serious about my work and wanted to live up to my reputation. I had enough sense to know that if I could win over the kitchen, the rest would be easy. On my first day of kitchen training I put on my apron and got to work right away, cleaning the area around the stoves, setting up bar mops just so, arranging the knives and getting ready to chop, dice and slice. The first sign of a good cook is how clean they work and how organized they are. A good line cook anticipates everything and sets themselves up early on so they don't have to be a burden on the rest of the team once things get going.

One day, soon after I arrived at Foggy Bottom, I was watching Jacqui make the peanut sauce for the Asian noodles. Starting with a jar of unsweetened peanut butter, she stirred in soy sauce, brown sugar and cider vinegar. Once well mixed and smooth, she finished it off with chili peppers and sesame oil, adding a slow stream of hot water to thin it down to the right consistency. Then came the tempura batter for the veggie and shrimp dish. She separated the eggs, reserving the yolks for the caper hollandaise sauce. In another bowl, she measured out the flour and added some cold water. She then poured in the egg whites and whisked the batter. She would dip the veggies and shrimp into this batter before dunking them into the hot oil, then serving. Once she had finished, I volunteered to do the hollandaise. Jacqui lowered her head and raised an eyebrow. "You sure you want to do the hollandaise?" she asked. I was sure. It was a reliable gauge of skill that any decent cook should have and a great way to impress. Jacqui watched me as I whipped up the egg yolks over a warm water bath, then slowly added the clarified, infused butter and whisked it all into a frothy, yellow, silky concoction. By the time the sauce was done, Jacqui knew she had a partner in the kitchen, someone she could count on. We were besties for the year and a half I was there.

Each night, right before the rush started, Jacqui would prepare her own version of ginger ale. She crushed fresh ginger and muddled it with lots of sugar then added soda water and ice. She kept a full pitcher handy in the reach-in throughout the night. The kitchen crew consisted of two more line cooks and a dishwasher. Everyone knew exactly what they were supposed to do and Jacqui didn't have to say much. Ten minutes before the 5:00 p.m. rush, head bandanas went on, knives were lined up, bar rags folded and set on cutting boards close by. The front of the house was called into the kitchen and presented with the specials of the day, which frequently consisted of a grilled fish accompanied by either pureed or sauteed vegetables and some sort of starch. One sample dish was usually prepared for everyone to try. Jacqui would describe the dish and, for my part, I would recommend the wine pairing. This was also the time to remind the waitrons to push certain items that might be nearing the end of their shelf life. For instance, if the scrod or shrimp had not moved well the night before, those would be "highly recommended" for the rest of the evening. Once the huddle was over, everyone would go back to their station and within minutes, we were rocking and rolling, knocking out the pre-theater crowd. There was no room for error or slackers. If you weren't ready, you sank like a cardboard ship in a rainstorm, and everyone knew it. The next day, you were gone.

I loved working in the kitchen. There was a sense of accomplishment and joy that came with cooking and conquering the rush. The kitchen crew were the stars and although my term was short-lived, I was now one of them. I had earned their respect.

The Foggy Bottom hummed like a well-oiled machine, and I would frequently come in early to help out in the kitchen before changing and overseeing the dining room set-up. We were open throughout the day but dinner was the key meal. We were packed with the Kennedy Center pre-theater crowd every night. They would line up outside the door and by the time

5:00 p.m. rolled around, we began seating. At 5:10 we had a full house. Our job was to get them in and out in less than two hours in time for the show.

Once they left, then came the real diners who lingered over their courses, ordered the best wines, and had time to share a dessert and a digestif. These were the big-time tippers. They were followed by the after-theater crowd. On many nights we would have the actors and crew from the Kennedy Center stop in after the show. They were gregarious and loud, and many stayed in character throughout the night, laughing and singing and generally drawing as much attention to themselves as they could. They were serious drinkers and often stayed way past closing time. I didn't mind it and I would sometimes be invited to join them. It was always fun to see some famous faces in the mix. On any given night, there was a star or two that could be spotted. Some were discreet; others came with an entourage and made a grand entrance, soliciting an ovation from their adoring fans. During my time at the Café, I saw Elizabeth Taylor, who garnered the longest ovation, Brad Davis, Jessica Lange and my favorite, Kathleen Turner, who, at the time, was on top of her game, having just come off of the steamiest film ever made, *Body Heat*. With her 5'8" frame and luscious curves she mesmerized the staff, including me. She was staying at the River Inn, the hotel that housed the Foggy Bottom Café, during the time she was performing at the Kennedy Center. Every afternoon, she would come down before the place opened for dinner to have a drink or a glass of warm milk with oatmeal before heading to the KC, where she appeared in a psychological thriller with Brad Davis.

I spent most of my waking hours at the Café. I lived in the Kalorama neighborhood, in a rent-controlled apartment, and walked the two miles to work every day and night for the next 18 months. On days that I had to open I had to be at work before 6 a.m. to get ready to open by 7. The place was small enough that even with someone calling out I was still able to get it going. I knew my way around the kitchen and all other aspects of the restaurant. I knew what to do the minute I walked in. Never dilly-dally at the beginning, you never know what may come up: A call out. A late show of a cook or server. A backed-up drain. Whatever. I had learned over the years to start setting up from the front door to the back. Make sure that the entrance looks inviting, the dining room is set, the bar ready to go, and then proceed with the bathrooms and the kitchen. This way, if someone calls out or is late, you can still open without appearing to be short-handed. You can always get to the stuff behind the scenes after you open.

On Thursdays I had to be up at 4:30 a.m. to pick up flowers for the week at the I Street flower wholesaler. I would select handfuls of freesias, gerbera daisies, forsythia, tulips or whatever was available. I learned a lot at the Foggy Bottom Café. Aside from cooking and flower arrangements, I especially learned that running a restaurant is much like show business. Lights, camera, action!

My stint at 209 1/2 and Foggy Bottom Café lasted a little under two years. I could see a whole world outside, but there was little chance of reaching it with the hours and schedule I had working as a manager in a busy restaurant. I felt like a moth trapped in a jar. At that point, I had bigger ideas. I just didn't know the details yet. I wanted to learn more about all aspects of the business and felt I had reached the end of the line with the Wollens. Jason and Rose were great teachers, but they left little room for creativity. Everything was regimented and preordained from the menu to the decor. To grow, I needed to get out. By then, I knew that I was a good fit for the restaurant business. I loved the work. The long hours. The exhilaration of a dinner rush. Watching people enjoying themselves and knowing I had played my part in bringing them joy. I also had all the right instincts, something I'd discovered early on at my father's restaurant. To this day, I am not sure that you can teach those instincts, since few people seem to possess them. They are the hospitality superpowers, and I can spot them when I meet a great server or hire someone who's really good. I know then that I have met a kindred spirit.

I also wanted to learn more about other aspects of the business. Finance, forecasting, payroll, and other technical skills. Often these are referred to as hard skills. As I saw it, there were two ways for me to get such training. Either I worked at a large restaurant group or hotel, or I went back to school. School was not a viable option since I needed to make a living. So, when I was offered a job at the Shoreham Hotel as an assistant manager in their upscale dining restaurant, The New Leaf, I jumped at the opportunity.

I was nervous about telling Jason. I knew that he would not take the news well. When the day came, I called to make an appointment. The first words out of his mouth were, "Are you leaving?" I was taken by surprise that he knew, since I had not told anyone at that point. He tried for a moment to convince me otherwise. "We are planning on expanding, you know. We are opening another restaurant by the end of the year and I was going to ask you if you have any interest in helping with the opening," he said. But I had already made up my mind and was starting at The Shoreham in two weeks. Once he knew that there was no turning back, he quickly changed his tune. "I think it's best for everyone if you just leave right away," he said curtly. I was hurt and sad and didn't want to burn such an important bridge. But Jason did not want a lame-duck manager, and he didn't want the last few days to be morale-busters for the rest of the staff. He paid me for the last two weeks and sent me on my way. I headed to the beach for a much-needed rest.

7

MOVING ON UP

The lobby of the Shoreham Hotel is a gleaming testament to opulence and excess. Soaring ceilings with heavenly painted scenery, huge indoor live trees, polished marble, sturdy furniture with intricate carvings. Everything about it says, "grand." Built in 1930, the hotel soon became the place of choice for Washington society. It had a legendary history that included the first inaugural ball of FDR in 1933 and every presidential inaugural thereafter. Every big-time act of the '30s and '40s and '50s was featured in the famous Blue Room. By the time I got there, Mark Russell, the pianist and political satirist, had a regular gig in the award-winning art-deco Marquee Lounge and sold out every night.

Working at The Shoreham was never boring. There was always something major and historically significant happening. A few months after I started there, Ronald Reagan's first inaugural ball took place. Weeks before the big day, each person working the event had their background checked by the Secret Service. It was quite a shindig, with more limos than a state funeral procession. Red carpets covered every walkway, paparazzi hovered in every corner, cameras flashed continuously. It was a heavy dose of Hollywood on the Potomac, complete with velvet ropes and movie star sightings. It was said that there were more stars that night than the biggest movie premiere.

Elizabeth Taylor and Charlton Heston were among the big hitters. Thousands of men in tuxedos and women in long, elegant gowns milled about, watched over by Secret Service agents in black with earpieces. Every ballroom and hallway was filled. You could feel the electricity in the air, and I was swept up in the excitement, making sure that the staff was on point and no detail left unnoticed.

There were other memorable moments working at The Shoreham. For instance, one night, Donna Summer requested oatmeal at 3:00 a.m., when room service had closed. I received a call from a panicky front desk clerk who had exhausted his options of finding a manager and was finally able to reach me. Luckily, I lived a few blocks away from the hotel and was able to dress quickly and jog over the Rock Creek Bridge to the hotel to make it happen. The oatmeal had to be served with seven raisins, not eight, not six, but seven. "Ms. Summer insists on the precise number of raisins," her assistant asserted. Ms. Summer was in DC for a concert at Merriweather Post Pavilion and had just returned to the hotel after the performance. I cooked the oatmeal from scratch. I knew it would take at least 30 minutes to make. I called Ms. Summer's assistant and warned him that it would take some time. He reiterated the seven raisins requirement. I used milk instead of water and a spoonful of honey for a touch of sweetness. I kept stirring the thickening concoction, slowly adding milk to keep it from getting too thick. I wanted it to be perfect. When it was done, I placed the raisins on top with six in a circle and one in the center. I delivered it myself with a small note welcoming Ms. Summer to The Shoreham and apologizing for the long delay. By the time I was finished it was after 4:00 a.m. and rather than going home, I got a head start at setting up the breakfast café for the morning.

Another night, Tom Selleck was spotted in the hotel. Word quickly made the rounds, and the entire staff wanted to get a glimpse. He was at the swooniest peak of his career, causing a frenzy among the workers, men and women alike. Housekeepers were sending messages as to which exit he was using, creating a small horde of hotel staff dusting ledges, vacuuming, polishing walls over and over again, waiting for the elevator to open. By the time Mr. Selleck came out, that corridor was the cleanest spot of any hotel in America. His tanned 6' 4" frame, full head of dark hair, dimpled face and perfectly trimmed mustache did not disappoint.

It was also at The Shoreham where I met my future wife. Marjan was working as a cocktail waitress at the Marquee Lounge and had been there for a few weeks prior to my start. After Mark Russell left, The Marquee became the premier art-deco lounge, hosting a full big band nightly, complete with trumpets, bass, violins and drums. It was the only club in Washington, DC, that had ballroom dancing.

It was during the company holiday party that Marjan approached me and asked me to dance. I was taken by surprise. Apparently, she had been plotting this move for weeks. I declined, keeping my professional decorum, and thought nothing of the encounter. Later, when a new café opened at the Shoreham, she asked to transfer from the Marquee. Again, this was her way of staying in my orbit. She worked there as a hostess, showing up at 5:30 a.m. for her 6 o'clock shift five days a week. She had a great presence and was an excellent hostess, being able to juggle a long line at the front door. She had long, cascading, dark, curly hair and a slender build and was sometimes stopped at airports having been mistaken for Cher. She wore tight-fitting dresses and six-inch heels, which never seemed to bother her. Her schedule did not allow much time for a break, and she would often work non-stop the entire eight-hour shift or more, walking back and forth on the unforgiving marble floor in those heels. She hardly took time off and never complained. I was impressed with her work ethic and her willingness to fill in anytime I needed her to cover shifts. She would later confide that every night she went home and soaked her swollen feet.

After a few months of working at The Shoreham, Marjan and I started a flirtatious back and forth. When I finally asked her out for our first date, it felt as though we had known each other for a while. We got married a year after that, during an afternoon break from work. I waited for the evening manager to arrive, then we jumped in her car and drove to the Arlington County Courthouse, where a justice of the peace conducted a civil ceremony. We returned to work about an hour later. We kept our marriage a secret for fear of breaking a workplace rule. By then Marjan, who was working on a degree in computer programming, was ready to leave The Shoreham anyway and pursue a career in IT.

I spent my first six months at The New Leaf, the hotel's upscale dining room. In many ways it resembled 209 1/2 but was more formal. The tables were fancier and covered with two layers of starched table cloths, the mood was more elegant, the china and glassware were imported and the Caesar salad was made in large, wooden salad bowls table-side. It was made into a show, starting with rubbing the bowls with fresh garlic, then adding the coddled egg yolk, olive oil, salt and pepper, whisking it into a golden froth and, tossing in the romaine lettuce. It was finished off with baked-in-house croutons, strips of anchovies and dramatic squeezes of fresh lemon. There were tuxedoed waiters, a maitre d', and rechauds, the copper portable stoves for table-side cooking. The general manager was a woman named Julie. She did not impress me, and I knew at first glance that, in no time at all, I would be taking over her job. Everything about Julie said mousy. Her hair, her demeanor, her voice, even the way she scurried about the dining room. She wore a company-issued one-size-too-big navy blue suit with a white blouse, making her look like a budget airline stewardess. Not exactly leadership material. Four weeks to the day, I was proven right. She quit.

I was fitted for a tuxedo, which I had to wear every day. It made it easier than having to get a whole new wardrobe for the job and besides, if I say so myself, I looked great in it.

My first day at The New Leaf had been in the kitchen. Paul, the chef, greeted me and showed me around, pointing out the various pieces of equipment. He was barely 21 and had a baby face that made him look even younger. He had come out of the Culinary Institute of America, the Harvard of cooking schools, and had the ambition, confidence and looks of a Top Chef contender decades before Top Chef became a thing. He even had a tattoo of a cooking knife on the inside of his arm. We hit it off right away. If there is one thing that kitchen staff like, it is someone who is not afraid to get their hands dirty. I knew my way around the kitchen and made it clear that helping out there was not beneath me.

I've found that when hiring for management positions in restaurants a heavy resume can often as not be a big red flag, especially if there is an overemphasis on degrees and certificates. To me, a degree in hospitality from Cornell, for instance, is a kiss of death. The people wielding them never work out for some reason. Cornell hospitality graduates wear designer suits and well-polished wingtip shoes. They walk around holding a clipboard, a Mont Blanc pen that they received as a graduation gift, and a stopwatch. They collect data in the hope that someone else will put it to use. The idea of getting dirt under their manicured nails terrifies them. Plus, they are the first to abandon ship when the going gets tough.

Job applicants who come in with a stack of certificates in plastic protective sheets in a loose-leaf binder should also be treated with suspicion. The binder will often contain some badly taken pictures of food samples and a photo of the applicant wearing whites and a very tall chef hat. They will refer to themselves as "chef." Often, they are sent by some government agency to fulfill an employment requirement. I once hired a "chef" with six certificates in restaurant-related skills: bartending, food handling, cooking, you name it. The person couldn't cut a carrot to save his life. He lasted six hours. Nonetheless, your odds of success with the heavily certificated are higher than those with a Cornell degree. The best applicants are ones who have done their share of grunt work. If they have not washed dishes, mopped floors, plunged a toilet, waited tables, bartended and worked the late-night shift, then their chances of success are greatly diminished. I have yet to see it proven otherwise. In my opinion, experience eats education for breakfast.

"I will be making a Béarnaise sauce for the filet medallion," Paul informed me, guessing I didn't know what a Béarnaise sauce was. "Let me do it," I said. He threw a crooked smile, handing me a French whisk. "Be my guest," he said.

By then I had perfected making this sauce. I gathered the ingredients I needed: eggs, clarified butter, lemon juice, salt and white pepper, and tarragon reduction, turning hollandaise into Béarnaise. Paul stood watch as I mixed the ingredients together. When I was finished, he gave me a slow clap. "That was pretty impressive," he said, grinning.

Paul and I hit it off and for the rest of the time I was at The Shoreham, I became the best-fed manager on staff. Each night he would whip up something delicious that I sometimes helped him prepare. My favorite was a medium-rare steak au poivre topped by a rich cognac peppercorn sauce, with mashed potatoes. The great food made up for the paltry salary that I was getting.

The New Leaf was also known for its ever-changing roster of dessert soufflés. We never had the same soufflé twice. The staff would come up with interesting flavors like peppermint chocolate, hazelnut and banana, and lemon with pomegranate. Customers had to order it when they ordered their entrée, since it took about 30 minutes to make. It was shared by two people and added a hefty price tag to the bill, which made everyone happy.

It was clear to the food and beverage director that he had found someone whom he could rely on. And so, for the next two years, I practically lived at The Shoreham. I had no life outside of work and my entire world revolved around a hotel that seemed big enough for me to grow and felt like a place for my dreams to take flight. I could someday become a food and beverage director or a general manager, which I imagined to be the perfect job. Free room service, free rent, no commute. What was there not to love?

A few weeks after I started at The New Leaf, Marc, the food and beverage director, met with the management team to discuss plans for a big renovation of the hotel. The New Leaf would close and make way for a larger dining room that would be more hip and less upscale to accommodate large conventions.

The new place was to be called Monique, modeled after the French bistros of the Rive Gauche. Omni, the company that owned The Shoreham, pulled out all the stops for this new concept, importing bentwood bistro chairs, etched tables, Wedgwood china and expensive stemware. The chairs alone cost upwards of $400 each. The floor was a patchwork of Portuguese marble of varied hues of brown, rust and tan veins. The walls were hand-painted *trompe l'oeil* of warm pink and gray resembling marble. Three French artists specializing in this kind of artwork were flown from Paris and worked at the restaurant for weeks. I watched them as they turned plain columns into beautiful pink marble using charcoal, pencils and paint, finishing it off with a glossy varnish. A new Bose sound system filled the room with the voices of Edith Piaf and Jacques Brel, transporting the place into a bygone era. Paul became the chef at Monique and was sent to Paris to hone his skills at French bistro cuisine. He came back with a whole new repertoire of cassoulets, choucroutes, entrecôtes, even escargots, which made the staff wince. My favorite of all was the *saucisse à l'ail* or garlic sausage. Two large sausages placed on a bed of sauerkraut in a covered copper rechaud. It came with a split of champagne. The champagne was then popped open and poured slowly over the hot sausage and sauerkraut at tableside giving off a head-turning, mouthwatering whoosh of steam and garnering oohs and aahs from everyone within sight.

Monique's renovation cost millions, going way over budget. It was the most ambitious restaurant Omni had opened in recent times, and I was excited to have been chosen to manage it. Within days, the top executives of Omni Hotels International would descend on the place from their headquarters in Boston. This was my chance to be noticed. I put everything I had into it, spending hours going over things with the staff, making sure that they could pronounce the items on the menu correctly and that they knew all the wines we were serving. I even made sure they knew the titles of the songs being played on the PA in case anyone asked. I wanted the guests to have a truly authentic experience.

Hours before the big kahunas arrived, I gathered the staff for a pre-shift pep rally. Hands clean, breath fresh, aprons well-pressed, three matching pens, wine opener. I looked around the room to make sure that all the salt and pepper shakers were lined up perfectly, the forsythia looked fresh and perky, the lighting just so, and Edith and Jacques loud enough to fill the space without overpowering it. Some of the waiters who had been there for years were a bit overwhelmed. Trying to pronounce choucroute or cassoulet was a challenge for those who had only ever served standard American fare. Within weeks of our opening, half of them transferred to other departments or left altogether. The ones who remained felt a sense of pride to have made it through the grueling training I had organized.

Over a period of three days the Omni executives were in the restaurant for breakfast, lunch, dinner and all hours in between. I hardly ever left my post during their visit and at the end they were blown away. Though I had no life outside of The Shoreham, it seemed to me that my career path was at last promising. Now I could really go places. When the Assistant Food and Beverage Director left suddenly, I knew that I was next in line for the position. If I got that job, I would be just a step away from being the director and then the hotel general manager.

When news came that someone else had been hired for the Assistant position, I felt betrayed. I knew that I was qualified and that I had worked hard, barely taking a day off for over a year and a half. I'd even slept at the hotel for days at a time when there was a special event. I had sacrificed a lot: birthdays, family gatherings, vacations. Despite feeling jilted, I kept my feelings to myself and tried to paint a positive picture in my mind. Perhaps the new Assistant was amazingly competent. Maybe the management had bigger plans for me at another property.

The new Assistant Director, Lorenzo, turned out to be a huge disappointment. He was an Argentinian with an accent and coolness rivaling Ricardo Montalban's. He looked more European than Latin. Within a few weeks it was apparent that he was incompetent and uncommitted. He showed up at events only when he knew he would be noticed, making a cursory appearance in his Armani suit, Hermes tie and Rolex watch, his thick hair combed back and perfectly slicked. He did little in the way of actual work and spent most of the time barking orders and trying to hook up with the waitresses. I tried to avoid him as much as possible.

Given his lackluster performance, I really couldn't understand why I had not been hired for the position. It stung. Although I couldn't prove it, I had a strong feeling that my ethnicity played a role. The only non-whites at The Shoreham were those in charge of housekeeping or security. Europeans had a lock on all other departments and food and beverage was no exception. There was little future for someone like me, an Arab with dark complexion and a short Afro. To move up, I realized, I had to leave.

8

MAKING THE SACRIFICE

The Food and Beverage Director at The Shoreham was sad to see me go. I had been a key member of his team. I never let him know the real reason for my leaving other than to go work in my family's business. Had I been promoted to Assistant Director, I would have most likely continued my upward climb in the hotel industry. Looking back, this setback was the best thing that happened to me. Sometimes things happen for a reason. Instead, I turned my gaze toward owning my own place. I knew, by now, that owning a restaurant was no cake-walk. With it comes a mixed bag of drama: backed-up drains; A/C systems that stop working on the hottest day of the year; ovens that malfunction on a busy Friday night. There are regulations to contend with, health inspections to pass, cash flows to juggle, payrolls to meet, and landlords who can be impossible to work with. Once you get past all this, you then have to deal with the two major reasons that bring about the demise of restaurants: theft and waste. Even a well-managed operation is lucky to clear 10% in profits. Most operate with single digits. There are restaurant tombstones strewn all over the world bearing the names of wealthy investors who thought, "Wouldn't it be nice to own a restaurant?"

Despite all that, I knew that with my experience and hard work, I could make a go of it. To me, failure was never in my cards. But my $25,000 salary at The Shoreham had not left enough room for saving. I was living paycheck to paycheck and barely staying above water. The idea of opening my own place seemed like pie in the sky. My only hope was my father. By then my relationship with him was so strained we hardly spoke. My family disapproved vehemently of my life's choices: getting married at 20 to someone four years older than me, and dropping out of my medical studies. Their dream of my becoming a doctor had been dashed. At 27, I just wanted to live my life doing something I enjoyed, and being a doctor wasn't it.

I swallowed my pride and went to see my father. I had to convince him to allow me to take over the old Pizza Kaezano. By then Ghazi had moved on, and my father had found someone to run it while my brother and I were in college. But the place was going downhill, and my father was looking to sell it. One afternoon I sat down with him and convinced him that rather than selling, he should allow me to take it over and turn it around. I knew it had potential, having seen it in past years. I also had some ideas that I wanted to try out. This would be a good proving ground.

We agreed on a deal that made him feel comfortable. Financially, it favored him heavily, but I didn't care. For me it wasn't about the money, it was about demonstrating that I could do this, both to him and, more importantly, to myself. With this arrangement I would have complete control of the menu and the day-to-day operations, which is what I was looking for. We agreed on a salary slightly higher than what I was getting at the Shoreham, and I immediately rolled up my sleeves and went to work, this time with an excitement that I never had felt before. The sky was the limit.

We served the last pizza at Pizza Kaezano one Sunday night and then closed the place for a month-long renovation. I was sad to see it close, having spent several years of my life working there. This was the place where I adopted a new identity and became Andy. Where I honed my customer skills. And where I learned the basics of cooking. There were so many memories hidden within those greasy walls. And yet, despite all the nostalgia, I was ready for something new. I wanted to erase all traces of the past and make the new concept solely mine.

With little time to waste I went to work right away. I could feel my father's gaze on the back of my neck. The fixed costs (rent, utilities, insurance, taxes, etc.) would still need to be met, and the clock was ticking. Each day without revenue meant going deeper in the red. I didn't want my father to regret making the deal. I wasn't looking for charity from him. I wanted to make this truly a deal between two businessmen, not a sweetheart arrangement between father and son.

I renamed the place Little Italy and found time to paint a large mural on one wall in the dining room depicting the Piazza San Marco in Venice, gondolas and all. It was cheesy, but it did the job. It was also a way to put my signature on the place. I hired a carpenter and oversaw the construction myself. He was one of the regulars from old times. The work was mostly cosmetic. A new counter, updated bathrooms, new lighting and new booths.

Then came the fun part: the menu. For the past couple of years, I had spent a lot of time in the kitchen at 209 1/2 and at the Shoreham Hotel, working with great chefs and learning a lot about food and cooking. How to make a reduction and a roux. How to thicken a sauce without adding flour or starch. Cooking *à la minute* and so much more. Now was the time to put that experience into practice for myself.

I wanted to keep the menu simple. A few dishes done well is much better than many done half-ass. The menu offered two types of pasta, linguine and fettuccine, ten sauces, including white clam, meatballs, a decent bolognese and mushroom. Dishes came with garlic bread made from a hearty Toscana loaf, brushed with olive oil and fresh chopped garlic, then toasted in the oven. I added a couple of salads, such as an antipasto with prosciutto, Genoa salami and Mortadella, plus a nice Caesar with anchovies and table-side-grated cheese. Then there was the World's Best Cheesecake. Boy was that delicious. It came frozen and cost me just $2 for eight slices. You took it out of the freezer the night before and let it sit in the refrigerator for 24 hours to thaw, restoring its creamy texture. I hated serving something frozen, but when it's that good, you have to just let it be.

The pasta was top-of-the-line De Cecco linguine imported from Italy and spinach fettuccine that was freshly made by Vace, a DC institution run by an Italian family. Vace was the authentic place for Italian specialty foods in the heart of Cleveland Park. I used to go there twice a week to pick up the fettuccine, try out a new sauce or two, and grab a slice of brick oven pizza for the drive home. The blistered-crusted pizza with fresh veggies and stretchy mozzarella alone made the 45-minute car ride worthwhile.

Right before opening I took several trips to SoHo, New York, visiting the small Italian shops there and checking out the latest trendy restaurants. I was introduced to tortellini, tagliatelle, penne and rigatoni right in the heart of Little Italy in lower Manhattan. I would spend the day hopping from one place to another. The day would begin at 6 a.m. with Bloody Marys in the train's dining car. By the time it pulled into Penn Station, I would be sporting a gentle buzz. My goal for the rest of the day was to maintain that steady buzz till I took the train back to DC at 6 p.m. This was no small task, since tipping over this balancing act would make the trip unproductive. I would visit upwards of six restaurants, trying out various dishes, beginning with breakfast, then a snack, then lunch, followed by another snack, then dinner and ending with dessert. I took copious notes, highlighting every dish—what I liked about it, how I might do it better and the ones I should consider including in the new menu. It was the first time I was introduced to tripe. Definitely not showing up on my menu. I also looked for trends in decor or table settings. Small touches like silverware placement, menu styles, using empty wine bottles for water service, using mismatched china and silverware. By the end of the day, on the way home, my belly would be stuffed, my mind energized, and I couldn't wait to put what I learned to use.

On one such trip I stumbled on a cute little restaurant in the East Village. It had a thick black velvet curtain at the entrance to keep out the draft, an idea that I would later use at Luna Grill and Diner. The place had no more than 30 seats made up of a handful of booths and bistro-style tables so tightly arranged that you had to be a contortionist to wedge yourself in. I stood at the entrance for a moment, waiting to be seated. A woman, thirty-something, wearing tight black pants and a denim shirt, seated me at a booth near the front door. Her reddish hair was a wild hive of curls that framed her smiling face. She jangled with bracelets and jewelry as she pulled a pen out of her hair. "Can I get you a drink?" she asked me with an almost cartoonish New York accent. "This is such a cute place," I told her. After exchanging a few niceties, she confided, "It's been a rough day, I had two people call out today and I'm running the show. Thank goodness my cooks showed up. I love my cooks, you can always depend on them." Then she told me to be patient and that her name was Donna. I told her that I was opening a restaurant in DC and that I was trying out different places in NYC. "Us Washingtonians are in awe about New York." We both laughed. She quickly returned with a complimentary glass of wine. This was my fourth drink of the day; I was already reaching my limit.

I sat in the booth and watched as people filed in. Within minutes the place began to fill up. First a party of two, followed by a party of four, then another deuce. People kept coming. Donna was playing host, bartender, server, busser, you name it. I watched her try to manage the impossible. The hive over her head was getting looser as she fell further and further into the weeds, pushing the loose curls away from her face with her forearm. Lubricated with liquid courage from the day, I decided to get up and help. Almost instinctively I started seating people and offering them menus, then quickly went to the bar where she was preparing drinks and said, "Hey Donna, I don't mind helping. I know how to do this. I'll just seat people and water them." She paused for a second. Her desperate eyes said it all. She was grateful. Getting our rhythm didn't take long and by the middle of lunch we were a team. By then my buzz had disappeared and I was shouting orders her way.

"Deuce at the window table, two Chardonnays."

"One club soda and a draft beer for the two gentlemen at the second booth."

"The booth in the back, three iced teas. Ready to order." And so on.

Lunch lasted for nearly two hours and died as fast as it started. When things began to settle down I returned to my seat. After Donna had finished serving the last party, she came and joined me for lunch. "Thanks for your help. You were like an angel from the heavens. Let me buy you lunch. That's the least I can do," she said. Within minutes one of the cooks came out proudly holding my lunch: flat, grill-pressed chicken, braised collard greens, pommes dauphinoise. The chicken was crisp on the outside and tender on the inside. The greens were vinegary and cooked just right and the potatoes, layers of creamy comfort. We laughed at what had just happened and she asked me if I wanted a job. I was grateful that I could help. We finished our extended lunch with two more glasses of wine, and I headed out the door well-fed and re-buzzed.

Back in Virginia, I worked day and night getting Little Italy ready, helping with the buildout, trying out different recipes. I even learned carpentry. I had to do it all and then some. Not because I wanted to as much as I had to. There was no budget other than my father looking over my shoulder making sure that blood was being squeezed out of every last turnip, and water from every last rock. My father did not believe in budgets. When asked about a budget he just threw it back at you: "What will it take to scrub the place and buy a couple of cans of paint?" He wanted details, not ballparks. Every penny had to be accounted for.

My father was the most frugal person I ever knew. He doled out money only after a long interrogation and although I never saw him write anything down, he remembered everything and kept mental records that rivaled most accounting software. He held his money so tight that his knuckles turned blue. I used to consider that as being "good with money," but now, recognizing that money is only useful when used, I'm not so impressed.

Within a few days of opening, word got out and locals flocked. I was the host, cook, manager, and sometimes a server when no one showed up. For months I hardly saw anything beyond the four walls of Little Italy. I had one other cook and a dishwasher who doubled up as a prep cook. Two middle-aged waitresses, one named Jenny who ran the morning shift and never missed a day. The other, Hanna, covered nights. I knew that the dining room was tightly run when Jenny and Hanna were on board. Jenny knew that lunchtime patrons needed to get their orders fast. Most had about 45 minutes for lunch. She wrote everything in shorthand and yelled out the orders to the kitchen like a marine sergeant. It wasn't *haute cuisine* service but the customers loved it, knowing what awaited them was delicious food that didn't require them to empty their wallet. Jenny knew most of them by name. When Reverend Wagner, the pastor of the local church down the street, didn't show up for his usual lunchtime pizza, she called him to make sure he was alright. She knew his schedule and he would report to her the days he was unable to be there ahead of time. Hanna had a different style: she lingered at the tables, and when a customer complained because it was taking too long for her to get to them she would soothe them with her charm. "Relax," she would say. "I'm gonna take care of you. I promise." By the time the customer left, they were best friends, sharing their kids' names and practically planning vacations together. Business took off like a rocket. Lines started forming for dinner soon after 5 p.m. From a value standpoint, Little Italy exceeded expectations on all fronts.

In the meantime, Marjan was working at Cable and Wireless as a computer programmer. We needed her income. She would come home around 6 p.m., change quickly and head to the restaurant to keep me company once the rush died down. She would sit in the corner booth reading or catching up on work. There was no laptop or internet to pass the time in those days, but she was a real trooper and felt bad that I had to work so hard. She wanted to be supportive, and I truly appreciated it. Sometimes she would help at the door, cashiering, or bussing tables when needed.

Aside from the long hours, Little Italy was an easy operation with little chance of failure. Concepts generally fail not because the idea is no good, but because of the execution. Often people enter a business with a tepid commitment. There are many ways to succeed in business. But the one sure way, in my opinion, is a willingness to sacrifice everything. And I mean everything. I have known many young entrepreneurs who want to enter the hospitality business. They often ask me what they should do to prepare for such a challenge. My answer is straightforward: Are you willing to sacrifice everything? Are you willing to leave your daughter's soccer championship game because the plumbing is backed up and a disaster is about to unfold? Are you willing to work for an entire year without a day off? I ask these questions not because I want to deter someone, but because these are my own experiences. I have had to do all these things at some point.

When Marjan and I decided to get married, I told her that our relationship would have to take second seat to the business. It didn't mean I loved her any less, it just meant that having a failed business would lead to resentment, stress and a failed relationship. To me, there is no such thing as work/life balance. The two are interconnected and the sooner I realized that the happier I became. Unless she was willing to accept it too, I would have been torn and would have been terrible at both marriage and business.

Little Italy was an original concept for its time. At least for Annandale, Virginia. There was no one in the entire area selling fresh pasta with sauces made to order, or as the pros call it, *à la minute*. Most Italian restaurants were doing thick red sauces that required hours of simmering and fussing over. Their food was rich and heavy and made you feel stuffed. Little Italy's food was lighter and fresher. Back then the word "pasta" was novel. Americans were beginning to learn that not all stringy dough was called spaghetti. They were also learning about sauces like pesto, alfredo, wild mushrooms, white clam, sun-dried tomatoes and so on. I kept prices to a minimum while at the same time making sure that quality and service were top-notch. The key, I discovered, was to exceed the expectations of the customer. It's that hard and that easy!

9

PLAYING WITH THE BIG BOYS

It was a year and a half after opening Little Italy that things began to settle down. No longer did I have to work fourteen hours a day or go without a day off for months. I had an assistant manager, a couple of dependable cooks, and a bartender. On many nights I hardly had to go in the kitchen and only stepped in to taste a sauce or help to expedite if things got in the weeds. Otherwise, I spent most of the time schmoozing with the regulars. Hosting. Helping out where needed. Business steadily continued to climb. I was proud of what I had achieved.

One busy lunchtime, a regular by the name of Bobby stopped in talk to me about a business proposal. I was too distracted with hosting and managing the floor, so he gave me his business card and asked me to call him when I had time. I wasn't sure what he wanted, but I was intrigued. We agreed to meet the next afternoon. He came in with a friend, also named Bobby. The first Bobby was an Italian guy. He looked like a character from *The Godfather* and for a moment I thought he was going to make me an "offer I couldn't refuse." He had black slicked hair and a short well-trimmed beard. He owned an Italian market in Centerville, Virginia, that sold imported Italian canned goods and frozen ready-made meatballs, raviolis, and a variety of pastas. The place apparently did very well. He told me that he had once owned an Italian restaurant in the same vicinity, but it hadn't worked out. He had been looking to buy a successful restaurant but needed to find a partner first. "Then Bobby 2 came around," he said, pointing to the other Bobby. They were neighbors and both dreamed of owning a restaurant. Bobby 2 was from New Delhi. He wore a suit and tie and worked in sales at IBM. He spoke fast and I detected a slight British accent. In his mid-forties he had saved enough cash for it to be burning a hole in his pocket. He was anxious to put it to work. We sat at one of the booths in the restaurant. I got two draft Bud Lights for them and coffee for me. Immediately Bobby 1 said, "Bobby 2 and I would like to buy your restaurant, are you interested in selling?" They had been coming here for weeks, scoping out the place. They loved the vibe, and the food, and thought it was exactly what they were looking for. They didn't want to start their own place; they wanted one already turnkey and successful. For them, Little Italy checked off all the boxes.

At that time, I had never thought about selling. First of all, it wasn't mine to sell. Second, what would I do? I had worked hard on this place and didn't want to just walk away. Third, what's in it for me? My father had full ownership of the space. But the idea sounded sufficiently intriguing for me not to want to say no outright.

I called my father and let him know about the offer. He didn't sound enthused. Why would he? He had a thriving business, operated by someone he trusted, generating a constant passive cash flow for him. For me, on the other hand, the thought of selling the business sounded exciting. I didn't want to drop the idea just yet. I went back to Bobby 1 and said that I was interested and wanted to get a sense of what was being offered. "$150,000," he replied. This was more money than I had imagined and a part of me wanted to scream, "Yes!" But I kept my cool and said, "That doesn't sound like enough, I'll have to ask my father. Is that your final offer?" Bobby seemed disappointed. "What do you think it's worth?" he replied. "At least $200,000," I said, thinking we would settle somewhere in between. I just pulled that number out of my ass, having absolutely no idea how they even came up with the $150,000. But I figured: Why not try? "I will have to speak to Bobby 2 and get back to you, but how about $165,000?" he quickly added. We shook hands and walked away.

I went back to my father and told him what had happened. Ever the skeptic, he didn't believe me. My father never imagined me as a businessperson. I was the workhorse. My brother was the business mind, who parsed the numbers and understood the way things ran. I resented every bit of this narrative. I loved the restaurant and the people and all the fluff, but I also understood the business. I had never negotiated a lease, nor haggled over prices for things, but I knew from watching and sponging that it wasn't rocket science. The real work happens on the ground. The "business" is the easy part that you can do at home with your family in the next room, the part that doesn't require you to miss your daughter's basketball games or your son's piano recital.

After a few minutes of discussion, my father seemed satisfied with moving forward. I couldn't help but believe that in the back of his mind he thought this was not really going to happen. But I was determined to see the deal go through. I wanted to have a clean break from my father and brother, and this would be a step in that direction. I could take my portion of the proceeds and invest in something that could be truly mine. I haggled over my cut should the sale take place. My father would take 70% of the proceeds and my brother and I would split the other 30%. That left me with about $25,000. It was more money than I'd ever had before.

I called Bobby 1 and we met at the restaurant. This time everyone was there, Bobby 2, my brother, and my father. After about two hours and several beers we cobbled together a deal, and within six weeks, I was standing at the door with the two Bobbys, handing over the key to their new place.

Now I had to come up with a new concept. I wasn't sure what it would be yet, I just knew I wanted it to be in DC. I was ready to play with the big boys.

10

SIMPLE AND SPIRITED

My first restaurant in Washington, DC, was called Skewers. As a concept, Skewers looked great on paper: a simple menu, easy to execute. A modern take on Middle Eastern food. The idea came from a customer I met once at Little Italy. She had just returned from Boston and had come across "the cutest Middle Eastern carry-out." She handed me a folded paper menu that she had picked up there. It had a picture of a shrimp, chicken, mushroom, and a chunk of meat on a skewer. The menu had the usual Lebanese dishes of hummus, baba ghanouj, tabouleh, maanek, (the small, spicy lamb sausages) and various kabobs: chicken, beef, veggie, and seafood, all served with rice. She told me that she loved the concept and thought it would work well in DC. I agreed. Although this was food that was familiar to me, I had never before cooked it and wasn't confident I could pull it off. I knew that the key to any successful restaurant was first and foremost the food. For a Middle Eastern restaurant, the rice would have to be perfect. It is the dish by which the entire menu will be judged. I called my mother to get her advice on making the rice. Her rice was always delicious and fluffy. "Make sure you wash the rice with cold water. Put some oil in the bottom of a pot and make it very hot. Once the oil starts to smoke, pour the wet rice on top of it and stir it well. Then add water to one inch above the rice. About the tip of your finger, no higher." My mother never followed recipes. Her kitchen does not have a measuring cup or measuring spoon or even a rolling pin. She relies on her tongue, her palms, and her fingers. She made the same things over and over again, yet her food tasted slightly different each time. If she didn't have cilantro, parsley was a good substitute. Wheat flour replaced white flour. Lime was substituted for lemon. These were subtle changes that added intrigue to her cooking.

I picked up a few Middle Eastern cookbooks and pored over recipes, picking the ingredients and combinations that made sense. Most of the items were familiar to me and fairly easy to make. You just needed a blender and a grill. The quality and freshness of the ingredients is what would take it to the next level. Tabouleh, for instance, can vary considerably depending on the ripeness of the tomatoes or the freshness of the lemon juice and the parsley. With baba ghanouj, you need good quality eggplants, picked early from the vine. The older ones tend to be bitter. And smoking them on an open flame makes a huge difference. There were a handful of salads with romaine lettuce, large chunks of feta cheese, seedless grapes and toasted almonds, and a choice of grilled chicken, beef, or lamb, marinated overnight in a dijon vinaigrette. I also wanted to offer fish options to emphasize the Mediterranean angle. My knowledge of seafood was limited, so I got a job as a line cook at a seafood restaurant at the wharf in southwest DC. I learned all that I needed to know in about a month then quit. Not the most ethical thing to do, but I needed to learn the tricks of the trade quickly if I was to succeed. Skewers was going to be my debut in the DC restaurant scene, and I wanted to make sure that I went into it with eyes wide open. Failure was not an option.

I brought in my father and brother as partners. Unlike Little Italy, it was a three-way business relationship with me in the lead. My brother and I would put in $25,000 each, which amounted to my entire proceeds from the sale of Little Italy, and my father $50,000. Profits would be divided equally. I took charge of the operation, and my brother would be responsible for accounting and filling in where needed. I accepted the arrangement reluctantly, knowing that I again would be doing most of the work.

My brother found the location: a three-story townhouse on P Street about two blocks from Logan Circle. With only a $100,000 budget we had to be very creative. I was responsible for the design and my brother for the renovation. It was mostly DIY. We hired day laborers and built the place with spit and gum. I bought used furniture and equipment and for the design relied heavily on color and fabric. I spent weeks picking out the colors for the dining room. I picked up a few copies of *Architectural Digest* from a nearby bookstore looking for inspiration. Turning the pages, I found a story on Yves St. Laurent's home Majorelle in Marrakech. An adobe-colored villa with deep blue and aquamarine accents. Eye-popping red hibiscus flowers surrounded the property. I took the magazine with me to the local paint store and picked out the blue that matched the one in the magazine. "Sequin Blue" was the name. The highlight, "Sea Foam." The accent colors, "Lipstick Red."

The colors were bold and modern. For art, I hung large white stretched canvases, and taking a brush to wet paint, I splashed them with the Sequin Blue, the Sea Foam and the Lipstick Red. The splashes formed colorful spots and streaks across the canvas and onto the wall. The result was a bit like Jackson Pollock but a lot cheaper. I tented the ceiling using sheer black fabric with gold embroidery from G Street Fabrics, remnants that cost me less than $100. Then, using a pair of scissors and a staple gun, I frayed the fabric and attached it to the ceiling. The track lights above mingled with the mesh material and gave off playful shadows on the walls that swayed when the fan came on for the AC. The result was an Arabesque decor that was sexy, modern, and whimsical.

When the day finally came to open Skewers' doors, I was ready for a flood of customers. Instead, there was barely a trickle. Hardly anyone showed up. I had prepped batches of hummus, baba ghanouj, and tabouleh. I had marinated the chicken and beef and prepared rice that would make my mother proud. I had the staff psyched and ready to go. I'd jumped through more hoops than a circus dog to get my liquor license. And yet: crickets. We didn't get our first customer until 7 p.m., two hours after opening. By then I had eaten three dinners myself. I hated to see all this food go to waste. The staff stood around trying to stay alert. Rearranging shelves. Dusting ledges. Just keeping themselves busy. I sat at the bar forcing a smile. Trying to muster every last ounce of enthusiasm to keep from surrendering to humiliation and defeat. By the end of the night eight other people wandered in. Sales were in the low $200s for the entire night. It was a kick in the face, a humbling experience, one that would be repeated over and over again for the next few weeks.

By the end of the first month, I was ready to throw in the towel. My ego was bruised; my bank account even more so. I found myself spending more time juggling bills than paying them. Business was not improving fast enough, and I needed a miracle.

In a state of panic, I decided to print flyers on the loudest color paper I could find: neon lime green. I hired a couple of neighborhood kids to plaster them all along P Street. This turned out to be a horrible idea. Minutes after they finished, I stepped out and looked. To my horror they had covered every light pole, every tree, every column in that hideous green. Every direction I looked, the street screamed. Before I could react, the calls started to come in. One irate caller after another demanding that I remove the signs. Threatening boycotts or worse. I was mortified. I ran outside and tore the signs down. I couldn't afford to be on the wrong side of my neighbors. I worried that what little business I already had would quickly evaporate.

In the days that followed I grew more and more distraught and wondered what I could have done to anticipate this. How did I miss this mark to such a degree? We weren't even getting regulars. Customers appeared to like the food and service, but did not seem wowed by the experience. I tried to engage people as Rose did at 209 1/2. For the most part, people are reluctant to tell you what they really think. Especially if you appear to be desperate. No one wants to tell you to your face when they look around and see an empty room. They just feel sorry for you, smile and tell you that things will be alright while knowing damn well they won't.

One morning I passed someone on the sidewalk who had stopped in for lunch the day before. He seemed a little drunk and loose with his words. "Oh, you're the guy with that new place that just opened. 'Screwers,' right?" he laughed. "Honey, you're cute but your prices are too expensive for this neighborhood," he slurred. It was a stab in the heart, but through his drunkenness he had made his point. That morning, I definitely didn't feel cute. His candid observation made me take stock. I knew that one of the things that made Little Italy such a hit was the prices. People expected to pay higher prices but when they got the bill, they saw a great value and couldn't wait to tell friends about this new find. Skewers' entree prices on the other hand were above average for the neighborhood, which raised expectations and made the customer far less forgiving. The word on the street was that you were getting screwed at Skewers, not exactly the word of mouth I was hoping for. I slashed the prices that same day.

Skewers sat on the second floor of a townhouse. In the first few days I spent a lot of time hiding underneath the staircase that led up to the restaurant. It was a cozy spot that I retreated to when I just needed to get away for a few moments. A place to contemplate what to do next. Occasionally I puffed on a cigarette. The idea of calling it quits and closing the place made several appearances in my head. It was there, under those stairs, that I got the most frank comments from customers. Although they couldn't see me, I could hear them talking to each other as they left the restaurant. I was getting feedback in real-time. The chicken too spicy. The rice undercooked. The portions too small. After each comment, I quickly ran back to the kitchen and made the appropriate adjustments. I didn't want to waste any time. Sure enough, the comments began to improve.

I also watched carefully what came back on the plates. The trash tells you a lot about an operation. I never allowed any food to come back without inquiring about the experience of the guest and asking them politely what they didn't like. Rather than saying: How's everything? I would ask, how was the rice? When pressed and asked for specifics, guests are more likely to give honest answers. I also stayed away from asking questions that have a yes or no answer. I am a glutton for criticism. To me, it's far more useful than compliments. I am not a believer in the sandwich approach to feedback—slipping criticism between slices of praise.

As the days rolled by, business started to pick up. But the improvement was not nearly as fast as I needed. I began to consider going out and getting a job to tide me over. At that point I was hardly making a salary. I was dependent on Marjan's income, which wasn't very much. It seemed that my vision had failed. What looked like a rock-solid idea in my head crumbled when it saw daylight. The few hundred dollars a day in income barely covered the rent. I wondered about going back to school and changing careers. I could always go back to waiting tables, I supposed.

Prior to opening I had sent a postcard inviting Phyllis Richman, the *Washington Post* food critic, to come to Skewers. She was revered and feared. Her name alone sent restaurant owners shuddering in terror. She was known to shut down restaurants with her icy pen. Her takedowns were legendary. Merciless. She traveled in disguise. Changed wigs. Sent emissaries. Her reviews even earned her death threats. Every restaurant owner and manager worth anything knew what she looked like. I had what I thought was a rare picture of her posted on the kitchen wall. It was hard to tell if it was her though because of the disguises she used. The only sure things were her height and size. She was shorter than average. Under five feet. In her fifties. A little plump. Everyone was on alert to spot her. On several occasions someone would come running into the kitchen shouting, "I think she's here!" Everyone knew who the "she" was, and everyone in the front and back would gear up only to find out moments later that it was a false alarm. This happened almost nightly. We all knew that a good review meant everything, while a negative one would have likely seen us close the door and call it a day.

It was exactly 45 days after we opened that Phyllis finally walked in. The miracle I'd been praying for manifested right before my eyes. Although I wasn't sure it was her, I had a strong feeling that it was. She was wearing a minimal disguise that day. We made eye contact briefly and I pretended that she was just another customer. Her husband was with her. Neither stood out in the least bit. They looked like an ordinary middle-aged couple visiting DC. I seated them at a corner table overseeing the entire dining room. My heart was beating so hard, I could almost hear it. My face was burning. I am sure my hands were trembling when I handed them the menus. I worried that she would notice my face turning cherry red. Or that I would pass out. There were four or five other tables of twos and fours in the dining room. Once I seated them, I immediately went to the kitchen and stayed there, tasting everything she ordered before it went out, making sure that every plate looked perfect. I had dreamed of this moment, replaying it in my head over and over. This was my shot at fame and fortune, and I made sure I gave it my all. I also made sure I gave the other tables equal attention. I knew she would notice these things.

Her first visit was followed by two more. Each time she ordered a noticeably large variety of items. Then came the wait for the photo and the review. Two days later someone from the *Post* called to schedule a photographer. In the meantime, debt continued to accumulate, and I continued playing eeny-meeny-miny-moe with the bills, making sure that at least the rent and utilities were paid on time. I was well aware that the review would be the turning point. It would mean success or failure. The three weeks leading up to the publication of the review had to be the longest weeks of my life. I kept going over every step of Phyllis' visits. Did she leave any food on the plate? Did she look happy when she left? Each day I would vacillate between assured confidence and panicked doubt.

The night before the review was due to hit the street, my mind was popping with anxiety. Doubt was winning. Sleep took a back seat. I lay awake in bed waiting for the dawn to arrive. By 4 a.m. I was too anxious to stay put. I got up, dressed hastily, jumped in my car and drove to the the *Washington Post* building in downtown DC, a good 30 minutes away. It was a balmy October morning. I sped through the slick, empty streets. The glare of flashing yellow traffic signals reflected against the wet pavement. I pulled up on 15th Street across from the loading dock of the *Post*. Through the fine drizzle I could see stacks of the Sunday paper under a plastic tarp sitting on the sidewalk waiting to be loaded onto nearby vans. My review, my future, was sitting right in front of me.

I stepped out of the car and approached a worker guarding the bundles. "Can I get one of those papers?" I asked. He replied with a curt "No! You'll have to buy 'em at the store." "Please," I responded, "I have a review for my restaurant in the paper and I was not able to sleep all night. I just want to get one magazine, that's all, just one." Maybe it was my eyes welling with tears, maybe it was my pathetic begging. Whatever it was, I was able to walk away with a copy of the paper. I thanked him and even offered to pay. He turned me down.

I went back in the car and sat for a few moments. By then I was a tangle of anxiety. I took a deep breath and gathered enough courage to unroll the newspaper and open the Sunday magazine with a deliberate slowness reserved for a high school senior awaiting a college acceptance letter. I peeked past the first page then to the second and on to the table of contents. "Skewers, Simple and Spirited," it read, and beneath it was the photograph of a skewer of shrimp floating in front of the lacy black and gold fabric. I quickly turned the pages and read the first few lines: "We haven't had a new Middle Eastern restaurant in Washington for a while, and we have never had one like Skewers. Much of what Skewers does could be done by almost anyone with a food processor and a grill, but few could make it such fun." I couldn't have asked for much better. The fact that Phyllis Richman thought that of my restaurant was thrilling beyond words. This was the mother of all breaks, and I knew right then and there that I was now part of an exclusive club of restaurateurs that had made it. I settled back in the seat, gave a sigh of relief and let a tear or two wash away my anxiety. I couldn't wait to share the good news with Marjan. She was waiting when I got home. When she saw my face, she smiled, knowing that things were about to change.

Many years later I told this story to Phyllis Richman. She was delighted to know that she, and she alone, was the reason why I continued in this business. Either way, had she not reviewed me, I would have had to close shop as funds dwindled and bills piled up. Phyllis Richman was the reason that I am able to write this story today.

That night business shot through the roof. We went from 20-30 covers a night to 200, which at first seemed like a blessing but quickly became a nightmare. I did my best to prepare by coming in at 6 a.m. and firing up the kitchen, marinating the meat, cutting the veggies, and getting the rice going. By the time 8 a.m. rolled around, the phone was ringing off the hook. I started to panic and brace myself for what was to come. Despite the amount of prep I did, the onslaught quickly turned into a massacre. It was as if the dam broke and we were drowning. By 8 p.m. we had run out of pretty much everything. We had to stop seating. I had no other choice. The next day I adjusted the schedule, brought in another cook, an extra dishwasher, more bussers, and called in Marjan and her friends to help host. This helped, but not by much.

The days kept increasing in intensity and, to make things ever more hellish, the following weekend brought in the largest gay rights march in US history. Nearly a half million people from all over the country descended on DC. Skewers became a hub for locals and out-of-towners wanting to try out this new place. Under any other circumstances, this would have been a gift from the heavens. But once again it was a clusterfuck. I remember that Saturday night as the march ended, the line started forming outside the door as people pushed their way into the bar area, which quickly began to resemble a mosh pit at a Lady Gaga concert.

Willy, a middle-aged Black man, was my right-hand cook. Prior to working at Skewers, he had never cooked this type of cuisine. But within a couple of weeks he got the hang of it. His rice was always fluffy, his baba ghanouj smokey and lemony with just the right amount of tahini, and his hummus was better than a Syrian grandmother's. He was a tiny guy with barely enough meat on his bones to keep from losing his pants. He was also very highly strung and needed blow occasionally to keep going. He was solid when he was on, but he had his days. He would disappear every so often or show up too wired to work. There was always something going on: His ex was after him for child support. Or someone to whom he owed money was looking for him. Once he called me from the police station asking for bail money. On another occasion his grandmother had a stroke, and he had to drive to South Carolina in a car he "borrowed" from a friend, which turned out to be a car he stole. The stories were colorful and entertaining, and I stopped asking too many questions. But when Willy was on, really on, which was about 75 percent of the time, he was the hardest -working cook I ever employed. He could juggle ten things and pump out those orders faster than a Tasmanian devil on speed. Willy lasted about two years. One day he disappeared for good. I assumed he had either died or been locked up. It was neither. Months later I got word that he had just drifted to another town to start a new life. Sometimes you just need to do that. Finding his replacement was difficult but like all things in this biz, nothing lasts forever. Just when you think all is smooth, something comes along to disrupt the apple cart. You have to move on. No reason to dwell. Like Willy used to say: "Keep it moving."

When we finally found our rhythm at Skewers, I was able to hold my head up and look ahead. No longer was I stuck in the kitchen 24/7. I hired more cooks. A manager. More experienced servers and bartenders. Occasionally, I had to step in full throttle but for the most part I only had to tinker: A problem with a cook. A manager having an altercation with a staff member. A customer who was irate and needed to speak to the owner. My role basically turned into resident psychologist.

On the first floor beneath the restaurant we opened a carryout: Skewers Express. It opened for breakfast and lunch and closed mid-afternoon. It became the lunch spot for the local non-profits, a place to get dependable ethnic food at affordable lunch prices. chicken or lamb kabobs. A rice dish with a different sauce each day. Tabouleh. We even had baklava courtesy of my mother's kitchen. The manager there, Michael, was from Trinidad and he would often whip up some jerk chicken special over rice. It would sell out in the first hour of lunch. We had a line of loyal regulars. Some came daily, ordering the same exact thing.

Our biggest customer was the Center for Responsive Law, Ralph Nader's think tank, which was just around the corner. Shortly after we opened, Ralph himself became a regular customer and would later become a close friend and ally. Being of Lebanese heritage he would stop in for his daily hummus, ful and other Middle Eastern vegan dishes. He also loved garlic and believed strongly in its medicinal value. He would order several cloves of raw chopped garlic on the side. After a couple of visits, the waiters knew to have the garlic ready. All they had to say to the kitchen was "Ralph Nader is here." On his way out he would frequently encounter a passerby contemplating coming inside. "The food is great," he would tell them, leaving them wondering if that really was Ralph Nader or a look-alike. It was enough to get them to walk up the short flight of steps to try out the place. I was grateful for his unsolicited endorsement.

The Center for Responsive Law or The Center, as it was known, was a hub of progressive lawyers and legal advisors keeping close watch on government. All day long their interns and staff streamed in, eating and meeting. These were the people who were working on changing the world. I loved having a front-row seat watching democracy in action. When Robert Bork was nominated for Supreme Court Justice, Skewers Express became a revolving door of activists meeting, plotting and depositing anti-Bork signs at the door after the demonstrations. Michael Moore, who went on to become a legendary documentary filmmaker, was a regular. He wore a Captain Kangaroo-like frumpy coat with saggy pockets and a tattered baseball cap with frayed edges. He was always in need of a comb or a haircut, or both. The first time I met him I thought he might be someone up to no good. He made a beeline to the open cooler case, grabbed some carry-out hummus, a brownie and some pita bread and shoved them in his giant pocket. I was ready to bust him thinking he was trying to steal the food. But when he reached the cash register he took everything out of his pocket for the cashier to ring up. I felt embarrassed to have judged this book by its cover.

Although Skewers Express was doing great at lunchtime, I was never able to capture much evening business. We were lucky to get a handful of people after the lunch rush. And as busy as it was for those two hours it wasn't enough to keep the lights on. I began to think of how I could activate the space during those dead hours. I tried dimming the lights. Pumping the music. Offering more substantial entrees. Nothing worked. The decor and layout of the place was hard to overcome. It was time for a complete overhaul, and I needed inspiration. I found it on the streets of San Francisco.

11

HITTING A BULLSEYE

In April 1990, I took a trip west to do research and see if there was something that might inspire me in finding a replacement concept for Skewers Express. California was a vast ocean of food and ideas and creativity, and I was soaking up every last drop. I spent a week there, visiting quirky Italian cafes, off-the-wall dives, ethnic places. The spot that I kept returning to, Café Flore, was located just off the Castro in San Francisco. The place was a hive of tattooed lesbians, flamboyant gay men, leather types and the rest of the world, woven effortlessly and naturally. The menu was written on a chalkboard, the bathrooms were unisex, colorful murals of peace and love covered the walls. A large shiny chrome espresso machine with levers to press the coffee hissed and sputtered. No matter what time I visited, there were people hanging out, making out or just doing their thing.

I came back with a binder full of notes and ideas ready to go to work. San Francisco gave me the spark that I needed. I knew what I wanted: something new for DC. Espressos, lattes and pasta. This was 1990 and DC was a wasteland of food options. An espresso was as rare as a cool day in August and pasta was only found at specialty stores or darkly lit fancy Italian restaurants.

And so it was that Café Luna took the place of Skewers Express. Much like Little Italy, it was a hit from the get-go.

Cozy, with just under 50 seats. The food was simple and well-prepared. Prices: cheap. Decor: not fussy. A red brick wall interrupted by broken mirrors and plaster on one side. A plain white wall for rotating local art exhibits on the other. I bought used furniture from a nearby auctioneer and a used six-burner stove and a large double-decker Vulcan pizza oven from a local restaurant equipment depot. I hired day laborers to do most of the construction. The whole place cost less than $75,000 to remodel. The biggest splurge was the La Marzocco espresso machine, which cost more than my used Renault. I made sure it occupied a prominent spot in the center of the bar.

Once in a while you hit a bullseye and this was one such time. Within days of opening, it became a hangout for locals. A place for people-watching. To meet someone for business or a date. It felt like it had been there forever. My work and planning had paid off. I had learned from my past mistakes and successes. But especially mistakes. Over the years I have come to embrace mistakes as lessons. To set my ego aside. And not let it get in the way of learning. If you don't make mistakes, you're not trying hard enough. This is an adage that has served me well over the years.

Rather than hiring a chef, I oversaw the kitchen. It was basically an updated, urban version of Little Italy. Individual-sized pizzas made with slices of fresh tomatoes rather than red sauce. Fresh basil and herbs with a slathering of garlic olive oil. Globs of fresh mozzarella cheese rather than processed cheese. Our most popular dish was a pesto lasagna. It was a blend of pesto and heavy cream, layered with spinach, mushrooms and three cheeses, baked to a bubbly perfection. I brought back the fettuccini and the linguini and the sauces from Little Italy. I wrote the menu on the wall, which was covered with blackboard paint, kept the bathrooms unisex, and played world music loud enough to be noticed. I hired people who worked hard and learned fast. DC hadn't caught the wave of coffee shops that were sprouting all over the West Coast. There were whispers of a place in Seattle named after a *Moby-Dick* character that did espresso drinks with foam milk. They called them cappuccinos. Lattes. They used words like Grande and Venti. It was growing fast and possibly coming to the East Coast. I wanted to get a head start.

Café Luna opened in the late summer of 1990. Saddam Hussein had just invaded Kuwait and the Gulf War was on the horizon. Being Iraqi, I was steeped in the whole mess. I followed the news intently and attended demonstrations opposing the war between shifts at the restaurant. The US attack started on January 16, 1991. I remember the night before. I had stopped by a demonstration in front of the White House after work. It was the most multicultural gathering I had seen anywhere. Every race, gender, age, and ethnicity was there. Dick Gregory was among those who got arrested that night after chaining himself to the White House fence. There were a couple thousand people by the time I got there. I could hear the beating of paint buckets and the blowing of whistles as I walked down 16th Street and onto Lafayette Square. Chants of "Hey hey, ho ho, we won't die for Texaco," and "Wake up Bush, wake up!" echoed in every direction. Someone was handing out vigil candles. There were dozens of camera and television crews present.

But, despite all the anti-war efforts, by the time morning came, the war had already started. An endless barrage of missiles lobbed from warships and jets. It was all over within a few days. And although thousands of Iraqi civilians and soldiers were killed, no one seemed to notice or care, at least as far as I could see.

Saddam Hussein had declared that Kuwait was historically Iraq's 19th province and was intent on reclaiming it. He even asked permission from the American ambassador to Iraq, April Glaspie. She gave the green light for the invasion and then threw him under the bus. The US government publicly appeared "shocked" by the invasion. It was right out of the scene from *Casablanca* when the police captain raids Rick's Pub for illegal gambling, saying he is "shocked, shocked," at what he has discovered, and then accepts a bribe to allow business to continue as usual. It also sent chills down the spine of neighboring Arab countries. Who would be next? Rather than ending the conflict diplomatically, the US quickly led the charge for a military attack. A UN coalition was assembled within weeks. Everyone knew it was just window dressing. UN coalitions tend to be just that. Within days hundreds of thousands of mostly US troops and all the military hardware they could corral were airlifted to Saudi Arabia. It was a war from the sky. No boots on the ground. Just bombs falling like meteor showers. The Iraqi army, then touted as the fourth largest in the world, was wiped out in a matter of days. Rows and rows of Iraqi military caravans with little cover disintegrated under this massive air assault. Aerial photos showed hundreds of mangled trucks and armored vehicles along a stretch of highway leading to Baghdad from Basra. Imprints of burned flesh could be seen against the twisted metal. It became known as the "Highway of Death."

The Gulf War set the tone for future wars. It made it seem so easy. Clean. Antiseptic. Much like a video game. For many Americans it exorcized the demons of Vietnam. And it showed to the world that America was once again the boss. Saddam Hussein played a starring role. He was a villain's villain. Ruthless. Camo wearing. And pictured carrying a large rifle held high with one arm like a guerilla fighter. The word "brutal dictator" became synonymous with his name.

Throughout, I didn't know which side to take. Invading an innocent country didn't seem fair. And I am no fan of dictators. However, I also know that when it comes to invasions and wars, no one is innocent. And fair is determined by who's on top. Hell, America invades countries all the time under the flimsiest of pretenses. Fair is never a standard. Take the invasion of Grenada, a tiny island in the Caribbean. Many Americans probably don't even remember the why or when of this war, but I do. The invasion took place in 1983. October 25 to be exact. I know that because it was just days before I became a naturalized American citizen. I heard about the invasion but didn't give it much thought until that day when I was on my way to be sworn in. Something about pledging allegiance to the flag without knowing what country we just invaded didn't sit well with me. It was a clear fall morning. The brilliant sunlight filled my eyes, and colorful leaves whipped and swirled about as I approached the large red brick colonial-style building where the swearing-in ceremony was to take place. A chill in the air made me forget Washington's sticky summer just a month earlier. All around me, people were rushing about unaffected by the news of the day. Grenada seemed distant and I felt guilty and ashamed not knowing where it was on a map. Back in Iraq an invasion would mean schools would close. Business would come to a halt. Government would cease to function. You would feel it somehow. But on that day in downtown Alexandria, Virginia, the war was nowhere to be found. No one felt a thing. And a part of me wanted to turn back, to call off the ceremony.

Grenada's main export, I later learned, is nutmeg. Nutmeg. Not oil or some precious mineral. But nutmeg. After the invasion, which was ominously named Operation Urgent Fury, Reagan joked at a White House Christmas function that the reason for the invasion was that we needed nutmeg for our eggnog, adding that it was also something to do with securing the safety of Americans attending medical school in Saint George's, the capital. The real reason however was hidden and had to do with overthrowing the Communist prime minister, Maurice Bishop. Within days of the invasion, Bishop was put on trial and executed by a firing squad. Mission accomplished. The media hardly questioned it and went along with the pretense. There was nothing fair about it.

Becoming an American citizen wasn't an easy decision for me. I am proud of being an Arab. An Iraqi. But that wasn't always true. At age 11, coming to America was quite a shock. Suddenly I was different. I stood out. Not in a way an 11-year-old wants to stand out. I looked different; I sounded different; I didn't fit neatly into a box. Not Black or white, as America insisted on every form I filled out. At every door I entered, I was reminded that I was the Other. The one America hadn't quite figured what to do with, so it threw me into a heap of Others. I tried hard to become invisible. To disappear. After all, I convinced myself, this was only a temporary situation. Soon I would be back to Baghdad with my friends and cousins. There, I wouldn't have to think about which box to fit into. In Iraq, there were no boxes to check. My wooly hair, brown skin, and name wouldn't matter. I wouldn't have to pretend that I was Italian, or French, or call myself Andy. I wouldn't have to change my name to something less foreign. People there knew how to pronounce my name. There, I could get my life back. I would become Anas again.

When I first arrived in the United States, I made fun of people who came here from other places and then called themselves American. To me, they weren't "real" Americans. They were just inauthentic wannabes: imposters begging for acceptance, for whatever crumbs might fall their way. Now I was becoming one of them. And like many of them, I did not swagger like an American, I did not sound like an American and I sure as hell did not look like one.

That day as I headed down the sidewalk into the courthouse to swear allegiance, I knew that America's sheen had already been tarnished. I had lived through the assassinations of King and Kennedy, the 1967 war between Israel and Arab countries, Nixon and his shenanigans, Vietnam and the deceit surrounding it. So much of America was lost. And now, getting ready to be sworn in, pledging allegiance to the flag, I was becoming one of those whom I detested. A phony. Trying to fit in. I pledged on that day that I would make sure to learn about Grenada. Learn about American imperialism. I would take my oath seriously and hold my new adopted country to the values it claimed to defend.

12

THE BUSINESS OF POLITICS

I once read somewhere that combining politics and business is a bad idea. But at Skewers and Cafe Luna I would prove this idea wrong. I not only combined the two at these restaurants, I did it openly and publicly. And made it work. My outspokenness about the Gulf War and other social and political issues was known to everyone. I made sure that there was no doubt where I stood when it came to American foreign policy, or gay rights, or capital punishment or women's right to choose. It seemed the more I spoke out, the busier we got. This was not a publicity stunt but a realization that whether you agree or not, people respect someone who is willing to take a stand. I had no interest or time for living in compartments. Life's too short. I worked and lived full-time and never bought into the idea of work-life balance, as if work is not life. I know people who work "normal" jobs and have nights and weekends off. They plan their vacations, their time off, their weekends, and they count down to retirement. From what I can see, they are no happier or more satisfied than I am.

But politics was where my heart was. The restaurant was my stage. So when I heard presidential candidate and ex-governor of California Jerry Brown speak at a conference for the first time I was ready to pour myself into his campaign. He seemed genuine. He had integrity. He was charismatic, visionary and spoke "truth to power," the first time I heard that term. Jerry spoke in snippets. Every speech he gave was a series of soundbites. He was always two or three thoughts ahead of anyone else. Tall, thin and wiry, he had a nervous energy that made everyone a little uneasy around him. Despite that, he was a firehose of ideas and knowledge, and I couldn't drink them in fast enough. At that conference, which was in the early '90s, he spoke about something called the World Wide Web. He talked about information overload. How too much information coming from various sources can result in paralysis. People would tune out. White noise, as he called it. He was prophetic in so many ways.

In short order, my home turned into the Northern Virginia Jerry Brown for President headquarters. People dropped in day and night to talk, volunteer, lick stamps, make calls, and plan the next move to promote our candidate. Meetings went well into the night. Fringe campaigns always attract fringe people, and we had our share. We actually did have a Joe the Plumber and a Charlie the Carpenter on our roster. Joe became a good friend, and I hired him to build a deck in my backyard. All I had to do was buy the materials. I was amazed at the dedication and smarts of ordinary people working so hard giving up their own time using their own resources to print materials, traveling for hours to conventions and meetings and standing at street corners and malls handing out literature. It's exciting to see democracy in action and the more I got into it the more American and joyful I felt.

Occasionally Jerry would be in town and would drop in at Skewers to meet with Ralph Nader, who was an advisor for the campaign. I looked forward to those days. Jerry was a treasure trove of ideas and often hard to keep up with. He would ask lots of questions, most of them rhetorical. Before you finished your answer, he was on to the next thing. Sitting with Ralph Nader on one side, James Zogby, the Arab American political pundit and founder of the Arab American Institute, on the other, and Jerry in the middle, debating the campaign and the issues of the day was energizing. The discussion would go on for hours weaving through the corporate takeover of the Democratic Party, the confluence of militarism, money, oil and tobacco, the lapdog media. I was a political junkie, and Jerry's visits became my fix.

I joined the Fairfax County Democratic Committee to work on the campaign. I never much adhered to party politics. To me, the party was more of a social club than a place to debate serious topics. The most contentious debates were trivial, such as the time that we spent over an hour discussing whether to serve corn on the cob or succotash at the annual crab feast. When it came to issues, there was little interest in discussing things that really mattered. It was understood that the FCDC was there to ensure that Democrats were elected at all levels and that issues should be left to the bigwigs at the top. There was little room for dissent and anyone who brought up inequality, or education reform, or spoke out against wars, was seen as a party pooper or, worse yet, a radical, God forbid. By Party standards, radicals were bottom feeders, too naive to understand what was important or just plain ignorant and misinformed.

Nevertheless, there were a handful of us who kept at it. We were more interested in upending the Party and making it accountable to its base. It was a tough line to hoe, and we met with fierce resistance that used parliamentary procedure, communication blackouts and other technical crap to ensure the status quo remained well-entrenched. Despite all that, our efforts managed to get a couple of alternate seats at the Democratic Convention in Madison Square Garden. An alternate is someone who is selected in case the actual delegate cannot perform their duties. I was one of them. I was told my chances of becoming a credentialed delegate were better than 50/50. And so, with my friend Paul Morgan, who was the other alternate, I took the train to New York on the eve of the convention. We got a cheap room at a hotel within a block of the convention center.

When we disembarked at Penn Station we immediately sensed that we were at the epicenter of democracy in action. The place around Madison Square Garden was a red, white and blue spectacle. Vendors were selling everything from political buttons to noise makers, bobbleheads of Jerry Brown and Bill Clinton, sequined T-shirts, Uncle Sam hats, you name it. Delegates of all sizes, ages, races were everywhere; there were even dogs dressed for the occasion. The newbies and the wannabes, the political hacks and the flacks. The opportunists and the diehards. This was a slice of Americana that I was all too happy to devour. It was easy to get swept up into the frenzied excitement. I felt like a child in a toy store. We walked around for a few hours and then made our way back to the hotel to strategize and figure out a way to get into the arena, where the real action was happening.

Uncertain about our status as delegates, Paul and I decided to look for volunteering options. One way or the other we were going to get a glimpse of the sausage factory. Our first volunteer gig was the evening prior to the convention opening. Stationed at the main entrance to the big hall, we were literally the gatekeepers greeting guests and directing them to their respective hospitality suites. This was the night when the big donors and corporate sponsors got to mingle with the delegates and the candidates. It was the worst kind of sausage making where deals are cut, and winks and nods are exchanged. Madison Square Garden became a cauldron of unsavory political stew, including Big Tobacco, Big Alcohol, defense contractors, auto manufacturers and anyone currying favor with the Party.

Big business doesn't play party favorites as long as their interests are aligned. Paul and I got a first-hand glimpse at how these corporate giants are treated. The higher the donor level, the more credentials were required for entry and the larger the shrimp size. Top donors received grilled or steamed skewered shrimp the size of baby lobster, along with passed hors d'oeuvres, real wine glasses, and a full bar complete with top shelf liquor. Low-level donors, meanwhile, got baskets of fried popcorn shrimp, chips and onion dip, paper plates and plastic cups filled with cheap box wine. Within moments of getting our assignment we recognized the absurdity of our charge and decided to switch it up a bit. We began to intentionally sabotage the whole deal by directing people to the wrong events. Big donors were getting the small shrimp, and small donors were directed to where the giant prawns were. This lasted for about an hour until we decided to abandon our posts altogether and join the party ourselves. To this day, I wonder how many disappointed high rollers we pissed off and what impact that had on the Democratic Party. Who knows, maybe there was a yet-to-be converted Koch brother who decided to switch allegiance that day. The guilt still weighs on me.

A day later, as expected, we got our upgrade to full credentials, giving us access to the main arena. Inside, Madison Square Garden was a circus filled with confetti, banners, flags, lights. The ceiling was covered with huge plastic bags filled with balloons ready to be dropped on the final day. It was brimming with Americana patriotic energy. Every seat was taken, every corner occupied. Men in suits huddled in the aisles. Delegates in colorful regalia made deals. Young interns darted about, carrying papers, delivering messages. There were people in wheelchairs, cowboy hats, hoop skirts, on stilts, even in clown costumes.

Food vendors sold popcorn and hot dogs. Throughout the day second-rate speakers of every stripe took turns at the podium. Few spectators paid attention outside prime hours. The main speakers, the stars of the Party, would speak later. Only then did the crowd settle down. The speeches became historic. And the frontrunner was anointed.

The final speaker was Barbara Jordan, the congresswoman from Texas and a powerful force in the Democratic Party. At least an hour before her speech, the place began to really fill up. People stopped milling about and secured their seats. Young interns guarded the VIP section making sure that seats were readily available for the Party's power brokers. Several speakers came on and off the stage with little fanfare, barely heard over the din of the room. Finally, Jordan was introduced from the podium. I had not heard her speak before but as soon as her name was mentioned the room fell into a hushed silence. She spoke for a long time, but people seemed to cling to every word. She admonished the party for not being more inclusive, setting out the dangers of leaving racism unaddressed. She closed her remarks by quoting Franklin Roosevelt when he rallied people from the darkness of despair during the Depression. Perhaps, she concluded, we were at the cusp of a rendezvous with destiny.

The crowd screamed with applause and the music played. I had no idea why, but tears were running down my face. All I knew was that I wanted this feeling to last forever. Democracy was on full display, and I was not just a spectator; I was a participant.

Going into the convention, I knew that Bill Clinton's delegates outnumbered all the others. Jerry Brown had a small yet respectable number, including me. It was not enough to have a big impact but sufficient to make a lot of noise and be disruptive. We couldn't be ignored. When word came that

Brown might not be allowed to speak, his delegates went ballistic. Chants of "Let Jerry speak" echoed throughout the arena. We wouldn't stop. By the next day, my voice was gone but my enthusiasm was off the charts. We had won. Jerry was given a slot. He was introduced by Jodie Evans, his campaign manager, who took the stage barefoot and wearing a long gown, like a flower child at Woodstock. I can't remember what Jerry said. All I know is that I was overwhelmed and filled with pride. I felt like a real American. It was a feeling that would come and go over the years.

Shortly after I returned to Virginia, I volunteered to become a precinct captain in my district. Having been bitten by the bug in New York, I wanted to be sure to keep my hand on the wheel of democracy. As precinct captain I was responsible for rallying voters behind the Democratic Party candidate. At times that was easier said than done: Democrats and Republicans were often a mere hairline apart. Nonetheless, I was there each election, waking up well before dawn and staking out a table at the proper distance from the entrance to the polling site and making sure that all signage and party paraphernalia was ready to go by the time the first voter arrived. I organized a roster of volunteers to cover the day and checked on them regularly, delivering drinks and sandwiches.

At the end of the night, when the last voter had cast their vote, I would huddle with the other workers at the precinct, including the opposing party representative, and count the votes. The results would be called into headquarters while everyone stood around the phone to ensure that the numbers were called accurately. It was exciting to see the results of at least my precinct before anyone else knew them. Being this close to democracy and seeing first-hand the dedication and commitment of ordinary people who clearly believed deeply in the democratic process was a humbling experience.

As much as I wanted Jerry to win, I realized that there were bigger things going on that made it impossible for him to get the nomination. Things he stood for like cutting the military budget, or talking seriously about poverty, or calling out racism, or not kowtowing to corporate interests, made his candidacy dead in the water. To the party establishment they were seen as pie-in-the-sky ideas, lacking pragmatism and viability.

Even before the primary and the convention circus, I had seen this first-hand during a fundraiser hosted by The Fairfax County Democratic Committee. The event, one of the largest in the state, attracted the would-be's, the wanna-be's and the gonna-be's. Even the has-beens showed up. Tickets went on sale months in advance. It was to be a huge crab feast held at the home of one of the county's biggest socialites, Dottie Schick. I was a regular volunteer there. Usually, I was in charge of one of the cooking stations. There were always more volunteers than were needed. There was even a waiting list for volunteers who had missed the opportunity of signing up early on.

Months before the primary, I invited Jerry to attend the fundraiser as an honored guest. That meant having a few moments at the microphone. I was excited to be the handler for one of the front runners. There was always a tussle when it came to who spoke first and last. The order was heavily scrutinized, and everyone held their breath as to who would be first on the mic after Dottie's introduction. The last speaker was usually the keynote. The big kahuna du jour.

Jerry flew in for the event. I picked him up at the airport and we went directly to Dottie's home. Several county police cars were parked with flashing lights, and cops were standing at each intersection around the house to direct traffic and make sure things ran smoothly. There was no place to park nearby. After circling the neighborhood a few times, I ended up parking several blocks away and Jerry and I walked to the house. It was still early but already a few hundred people had gathered. When they saw Jerry, people rushed to shake his hand. I stood by his side as he made his way through the crowd of well-wishers. A handful of people stayed at the driveway entrance to the house asking him questions about corruption in politics, the influence of big money, Big Pharma, the oil industry, militarism.

Jerry was not one to make small talk and, once the conversation on issues came to an end, he was ready to move on. As we entered the backyard where the real action was, we were met with a rush of people heading to the front of the house. Cameras came out and people bumped past Jerry giving him a cursory "hello" on their way to see what was going on. Three limos had pulled up to the front of the house. Out jumped men in dark suits with earpieces and sunglasses looking like the viruses from The Matrix. They stood around the limos scanning the crowd. A driver opened the passenger door and out came a tanned, polished, ready-for-prime-time Bill Clinton. He looked like an older version of a Ken doll. Cameras started flashing. People were swooning. Shouts of "Bill, BILL!" filled the air. It was as if Mick Jagger had just parachuted in. The bodyguards kept the crowd, which by then had become close to hysterical, at bay.

Jerry stood beside me, watching the spectacle of paparazzi and stage wizardry unfold before his eyes. I felt embarrassed and angry at the hoopla that Clinton was getting. This was way before any of the major primaries had happened and Clinton was trailing Jerry and others in the field. Already a formidable lineup of women had come forward in public, recounting tawdry encounters with him. He moved through the crowds slowly, stopping to hold the hand of each person. He seemed to pause a bit longer at the women. My mother was among those who fell under the spell of the Clinton charm. He looked her straight in the eyes and, in his soft Arkansas drawl, said, "Thank you for coming. It's so nice to meet you." I watched my mother being verbally groped and turning into mush. She appeared to be close to passing out.

Once he was finished shaking just about everyone's hand, he was whisked away into the main house where he disappeared until it was time for him to close out the speakers. It was an eye-opening moment. Politics is theater and requires staging. Jerry's entrance was barely noticed. He melded into the background. No paparazzi. No secret service-looking men with earphones. No limo or even a reserved parking spot. He was just another ordinary attendee to a fundraiser chewing on a corn on the cob and talking to anyone willing to listen. It was such a stark contrast to Clinton's entrance and entourage. It was already becoming clear that Jerry Brown was not going to be the nominee. Money was pouring like an open spigot into the Clinton camp, leaving all the other candidates in the dry dust. One by one they dropped out.

Jerry continued to make periodic visits to DC, meeting again with his kitchen cabinet, which I was lucky enough to be a part of. We would often gather at Skewers and discuss the future of the Democratic party, the influence of money on elections and a myriad of other civic issues. Ralph Nader, always the visionary, chimed in about the electorate being uninformed. The Center for Responsive Law had shown repeatedly that money had tremendous influence in elections. We needed to have a more direct line to the people. Actual physical spaces located in malls or other public spaces where ordinary Americans gather. Jerry, like Ralph, was an optimist. He believed in people and knew that once informed, they would know to do the right thing.

I suggested casually that we could start right where we were already meeting, at the space above Skewers and Café Luna. The third floor of the building was not being utilized for anything other than storage. I suggested that I convert that space into a small bookstore containing books that deal with politics and social issues. I would get a coffee machine. We would provide a small selection of sandwiches and desserts and some comfortable seating.

That was the beginning of Luna Books and Democracy Center and the planting of the first seed for what would become Busboys and Poets. It was a big title for a small, yet ambitious space. I spent the next few days clearing out the junk, scrubbing the floors and painting walls. We built a counter and some bookshelves and bought a used cash register, a display refrigerator and tables and chairs at an auction. The total cost was under $2,000. I filled the display refrigerator with pastries from a local baker and vegan cookies made with oatmeal, walnuts and chocolate. The menu was small, relying on food from Skewers below.

Next, I needed books to fill the shelves. They came courtesy of Ralph Nader's Center. The Center was filled with piles and boxes of titles that had been given to Ralph, including books that he himself had written. John Richard, the director of the Center, generously offered to donate them to us, free of charge. All we had to do was move them over to our place. Boxes were stacked near the door of the Center and on the next Saturday morning a human chain of interns made a line from the Center to the bookstore. The boxes were passed from one to another making their way to the third floor of the townhouse where Luna Books was located. I was there to receive them and within a few hours we had a room full of books: great titles like *Unsafe at Any Speed, The Civics Reader, The Hidden History of*

Monopolies and hundreds of others. A friend helped categorize and label the books.

Within days, word was out about this tiny hidden bookstore that attracted interesting people. Ralph made Luna Books and Democracy Center his home away from home, hosting interviews and other meetings there. People saw him going in and out of the place at all hours of the day. His hummus with ful and chopped garlic was ready for him before he sat down. Over the years it became a hub for visiting authors and politicians to meet with small groups of activists on almost every social justice issue.

This wasn't quite the model that Ralph had imagined but it served a similar purpose: a gathering place for advocates of social change to engage with one another and turn ideas into action. Ralph was a magnet for movers and shakers and dreamers, and a year after Luna Books and Democracy Center opened, he drew in a visionary who would change my life forever.

13

A PEOPLE'S PLAY

In the summer of 1993, Ralph Nader asked me to host an event at Luna Books and Democracy Center with the-well known historian, professor, playwright and activist Howard Zinn. Zinn was the author of the widely acclaimed A *People's History of the United States,* which sat prominently on the bookshelves at Luna Books. It was in fact the best-selling book we carried. I had never met Howard, but I had read *A People's History* a few years earlier. It was a paradigm-shifting book that changed how I saw history and the way it was told. Howard would say, it's not what you tell that matters, it's what you leave out. And much is left out in the history books that I grew up reading. We learn about heroes and change-makers without contextualizing their ascent, so that Martin Luther King is seen as a dreamer and Rosa Parks as an ordinary woman acting on her own. The reality is far different. Each one of those heroes had a movement lifting them up. King had people who guided him and gave him legal advice, who bailed him out and fought for his freedom when he was jailed. The same was true for Rosa Parks whose defiant stance and the Montgomery bus boycott it sparked was part of an orchestrated effort to desegregate the bus system in Alabama. The work took years of planning and organizing.

I admired Zinn's work and knew that he had a following among activists but, on the night he was scheduled to speak at Luna Books, I wondered if enough people would show up. As it turned out, I needn't have worried. People started arriving an hour before the event. Soon more than a hundred were crammed into a space that only seated forty, and a long line was forming outside. People were sitting on the floor, the windowsills, steps, you name it. A fire marshal would have had a fit.

Just after 7 p.m. Howard came up the stairs followed by his wife Roz. They were a handsome couple. Howard was tall and slim with a slightly bent physique and thick, white hair, and Ros had a graying ponytail, tightly pulled back. There was a dignified air about them both. Applause from people outside could be heard coming up the stairs, becoming a thunderous ovation as they made their way up. Howard smiled widely and slowly made his way near the front, nodding hellos and carefully stepping around people sitting on the floor. When things quieted down, I introduced him as an American icon and said a few words that didn't come out as I had envisioned. I was new at this and very nervous, stumbling and stuttering over words. I wished I had rehearsed. Thankfully people were not there to listen to me.

Howard walked up to the podium and the room quickly fell silent. The people at the bottom of the stairs couldn't see him but listened intently for what he was about to say. Roz sat on the floor in the front, hugging both knees and looking on. He began by cracking a few jokes, something to the effect of, "Why so much applause? Maybe you were expecting someone else." Howard was known for his self-deprecating humor. He then got serious, speaking of history as a tool to look into the future. Knowing history helps to put things in perspective and predict what's to come. I was in awe, watching as he poured out a flood of deep, fascinating ideas. I wasn't the only one. The entire room was mesmerized by his staccato delivery. Here was the historian who changed the way we see and study history. Who told history through the eyes of ordinary people sometimes working against all odds to change the world. He told us that it was the small wins that, over time, could change the course of history, that made it possible for him to see a rosier picture of the future.

When the talk ended nearly two hours later, the crowd gathered around him for a handshake or a signed copy of A *People's History*. Some brought their own heavily used, dog-eared copies. I watched from a distance, taking in the moment. By 11 p.m. the place had finally emptied out and I was left with just Howard and Roz. I had to pinch myself. We sat at a corner table, and chatted for a while over cups of herbal tea and oatmeal chocolate cookies—a favorite dessert at Luna Books.

During the conversation, Howard told me he was writing a play about Karl Marx. He did not want it to be didactic. The premise was that Karl Marx gets a dispensation from the gods in Heaven to return to Earth to clear his name. He has witnessed the fall of the Soviet Union and its aftermath. The fact that the world is regarding this as a failure of communism angers Marx. He never agreed with Stalin's version of communism. The political system so closely linked to Marx's name was not a dictatorship with mass executions and prisons. Stalinism benefited a few and left many discouraged and disenfranchised. Marx had much work to do to "right" history.

To make the story humorous and less dogmatic, Howard added a twist. Due to a bureaucratic error in Heaven, rather than Marx being returned to Soho, London, where he lived out his final years, he is sent to SoHo, New York. He lands there and enters a theater with an audience. He acts surprised and feels compelled to share his vision with the unsuspecting theatergoers. He begins to tell them about what he thinks of modern-day economics, capitalism and the Soviet Union and explains communism in terms that are funny and insightful. "You call this progress, because you have motor cars and telephones and flying machines and a thousand potions to make you smell better? And people are sleeping on the streets?" he questions the audience. Howard believed that sometimes you need to reach people where they are. He saw theater as a vehicle for conveying important concepts in an easily digestible form.

Howard's plan was to finish writing the play in the next year or so and then find a theater to produce it. Even though I had never produced a play or even knew what it would entail, the idea of working side by side with *the* Howard Zinn was too good to pass up. By the end of the conversation, I volunteered to be the first producer of what became known as *Marx in SoHo*. Howard didn't care about royalties, legal contracts or monetary arrangements. He didn't want to complicate things. He just wanted the play to reach as many people as possible.

The next day, before returning to Boston, Howard stopped by the bookstore and delivered a first draft of the play in a manila envelope. "Here," he said, "read it and let me know what you think." We sat at Skewers and had lunch: hummus and baba ghanouj and ful with plenty of warm pita bread. He and Roz tried the lentil soup. "It's my mother's recipe," I told them. It was nice and thick with plenty of cumin, topped off with a crispy burnt onion garnish, giving it a smoky, sweet taste. Sometimes I like adding a dash of sherry vinegar for an extra kick. Howard took a spoonful, slurping it slowly. "Tell your mother I like her soup," he said with a warm smile.

I started reading the play the minute he left. I made sure that I underlined the things I liked and the things that needed clarification. I made lots of notes in the margins. I wanted my comments to be smart and thoughtful, not sycophantic. I made copies of the marked-up version and put it in the mail straightaway. Howard called me the day he received it and we spoke for about an hour. He said he wanted to make sure that the humor stood out. He wanted the audience to laugh and not feel they were being lectured to. I tried out the lines on a few people to make sure they landed as intended.

We continued the back and forth for months. He would rewrite, I would mark the script up and we would talk again. On occasion, he would come to visit my home in Annandale, Virginia. My daughters Laela and Nina got to know him, sharing breakfast with him before going off to school. Years later, when Nina was in high school, she was assigned *A People's History* to read. She told the teacher that she knew Howard, and that he had stayed at our house. She reported that the teacher looked at her like she was crazy, not sure whether to believe her or not.

When the play was finished, Howard came to DC to check out the theater where we were presenting it. I had placed an ad in the *Washington Post* theater section looking for a director. There was a variety of great applicants to choose from, many veterans of the DC theater scene. Once the director was chosen, we quickly began the auditions for the one-man play. Howard wanted to be involved in every step. For two days we reviewed one applicant after another while sitting in the darkened theater taking only short breaks for lunch or to stretch our legs. The director Norman gave his input. Howard and I reviewed his recommendations and made some of our own. We worked with consensus. Toward the end of the second day after looking over at least two dozen actors we settled on a burly man with a husky voice named Will. He was one of the last to do a reading. He had done one-man plays and had Marx down to a tee. He had a scruffy beard and a large belly. He wore suspenders and a worn-out jacket. He didn't need much in the way of makeup or costume. He *was* Karl Marx. Now we had to get to work and make Howard's words come to life.

The next six weeks before opening night were filled with rehearsals and weekly check-ins by Howard to see progress. There were lots of pizza and sandwiches, courtesy of Skewers and Café Luna. Howard seemed pleased with the progress. And I was ecstatic about having a front-row seat with someone I admired and respected so much. Having my opinion solicited by Howard Zinn: what an honor.

The Church Street Theater was a 120-seat venue near Dupont Circle. It was the perfect venue for the play. With minimal staging and lighting we were able to pull it off. It just needed to look like a theater backstage with some spotlights here and there and a few sound recordings. The play was sold out for the entire weekend. Howard and Roz came to town as did many other civil rights and labor celebrities. I was usher and host, and frequently doubled as engineer in the light booth once everyone was seated and the doors were closed. Howard attended all five performances, taking a bow for the standing ovation that inevitably came with every show. I stood next to him, basking in his bigger-than-life shadow. Little did I know that this would go on to become a lifelong friendship.

Two years after I met Howard, he informed me that he was working on a memoir. He titled it *You Can't Be Neutral on a Moving Train*, a phrase he used at the beginning of each of his lectures at Boston University, dispelling the idea that telling history is an objective exercise. Every story told, retold and untold comes with a perspective. The book was an autobiography spanning nearly five decades of civil rights activism and teaching. He asked me if I would host the book launch at Luna Books. I jumped at the opportunity. We set a date and, once I received the book, I went to work planning the event. I read it once and then re-read it. I came to appreciate Howard Zinn more than ever. He wasn't just recording history, he himself had been at the center of it. An active participant who made an enormous impact on the civil rights movement and how people understood history. He touched the lives of lots of people, many of whom made an appearance in the book. I took a yellow highlighter and began to mark any mention of any name whose life was in any way changed by Howard's work. After being fired from Boston University he taught at Spelman College. There he touched the lives of Alice Walker, the Pulitzer Prize-winning author of *The Color Purple*, Mariam Wright Edelman, founder of The Children's Defense Fund, and Bernice Johnson Reagon of the singing group Sweet Honey in the Rock. They were students at Spelman and later influenced an entire generation of young Black women. There was also Julian Bond, whom Howard marched with in Atlanta, and Ron Kovic, who became an outspoken critic of the war after coming back from Vietnam. He was confined to a wheelchair for the rest of his life having suffered a nearly fatal injury during the war. Ron wrote one of the best anti-war novels, *Born on the Fourth of July*, which was later made into a film by Oliver Stone starring Tom Cruise. And Daniel Ellsberg, who hid in Howard Zinn's home while evading the FBI after releasing the Pentagon Papers.

I wanted the memoir launch to be something special, befitting its author. With a bit of sleuthing, I was able to find contact information for most of the people referenced in the book. I remember calling Alice Walker. I was surprised when she answered the phone herself. I quickly recovered and invited her to attend the book event. She was thrilled to be asked and although she couldn't attend in person, she was willing to phone in. Ron Kovic was also unable to travel but said he would call at a certain hour during the evening. Many of the others, such as Julian Bond, Mariam Wright Edelman and Bernice Johnson Reagon, were close by and promised to attend.

As the day approached, I made sure we had plenty of champagne on hand. I sent out the invitations and readied the bookstore for the occasion, making sure to maximize the seating and reserve spaces for special guests. I made plenty of lentil soup, by now Howard's favorite, and a buffet of hummus, baba ghanouj and tabbouleh. And I made sure that Howard's books were prominently displayed.

I asked everyone to come an hour before the start time. I was planning a surprise for Howard. Not just an ordinary book reading but something memorable for him and for the hundred or so people who crammed into the bookstore. This was an invitation-only event made up of a who's who of the civil rights movement. People arrived early and sat wherever they could find a space. Bernice Johnson Reagon sat on a stool that was reserved for Howard. At the time I didn't recognize her and asked that she please move to a less prominent seat. Boy was that a mistake. She responded to me in no uncertain terms that she was not moving. Her stare alone burned a hole in my center. When I heard her voice, I realized who it was. I felt terrible and apologized profusely. I was met with a glare. When I ran into her months later at a concert, I was worried that the burning stare might return, but happily she seemed to have forgotten about the slight and was perfectly gracious.

When Howard arrived, I made sure the people whom he mentioned in the book were hidden from sight. Once he was settled, they all came out together in a group and surprised him. He hugged each of them and thanked them for coming and me for making it happen. I felt so proud. Then Bernice opened the program with a rendition of a song inspired by Ella Baker's 1964 speech, "We who believe in freedom cannot rest," while tapping the podium with her palm. This was a real treat.

She was at the top of her game—Sweet Honey in the Rock was selling out large concert halls. She spoke in a low cadence about how Howard Zinn was able to challenge the isolation of Spelman during the civil rights movement, leading students into demonstrations and encouraging them to break the rules if necessary to bring about change. Change is never given, it has to be fought for, she said.

Next up, Alice Walker called at the agreed-upon time. I set the receiver beside a microphone. The warmth of her affection for Howard came through from 3,000 miles away. She recalled the days at Spelman when Howard encouraged her and other students to break the rules and join the civil rights movement. Soon after Alice hung up, Ron Kovic called. He was sitting in a café in Sausalito, California. His eloquence was extraordinary despite the background noise. He spoke about the impact that Howard had on him and his journey from warrior to peace activist. He spoke of how our government lied to get into the war in Vietnam and how many were killed or injured. By the end of his 15-minute monologue, everyone was moved to tears, including Howard and Roz. The stories went on, well into the night. Back then, there were no cell phones or social media, and recording events required a great deal of effort. But I wish I had a record of that night.

What impressed me the most about Howard Zinn was his sense of hope. He had seen and written so much yet he believed in ordinary people accomplishing extraordinary things. My favorite quote of his, a guiding principle that I have often turned to in times of despair, is as follows:

> To be hopeful in bad times is not just foolishly romantic. It is based on the fact that human history is a history not only of cruelty, but also of compassion, sacrifice, courage, kindness.

What we choose to emphasize in this complex history will determine our lives. If we see only the worst, it destroys our capacity to do something. If we remember those times and places–and there are so many–where people have behaved magnificently, this gives us the energy to act, and at least the possibility of sending this spinning top of a world in a different direction.

And if we do act, in however small a way, we don't have to wait for some grand utopian future. The future is an infinite succession of presents, and to live now as we think human beings should live, in defiance of all that is bad around us, is itself a marvelous victory.

That night at Luna Books and Democracy Center was, indeed, a marvelous victory.

14

GOING SOLO

After Howard Zinn's book launch, I knew that I was on to something. People raved about the event for weeks afterwards. This wasn't just a book talk, it was a way of bringing history to life. The people in that room that night were some of the most influential people in the civil rights movement, the people who work tirelessly to make the planet more livable. I made sure I thanked all those who attended, and being that many were well-known writers, I invited them back for a reading or a book signing for themselves. To my surprise, almost every one of them agreed and many of them remain friends to this day. The seed had been planted for future events and I went on to host evenings with Alice Walker, Angela Davis, Nikki Giovanni, Harry Belafonte, Colman McCarthy, John Lewis, Wangari Mathaai, Jesse Jackson, Marion Barry and many others. Each occasion was memorable. And each created a ripple effect for future events.

By now I was doing these types of events several times a month. Those nights were magical. I started thinking more and more about how to take Luna Books and Democracy Center beyond the confines of the third floor. As much as I loved the intimacy of the space, it was too small and inaccessible. For many events, I was turning away more people than we could fit inside.

I was aware that my father and my brother, my business partners, were not as excited about the events as I was. They knew the events were helping the business grow, but they were much more focused on the revenue generated than what was happening in the space. Revenue was important, but my main interest was something bigger. I wanted to provide a platform for the ideas and voices of the wonderful people appearing in the space to resonate.

Our divergent ideas began to take their toll on our family relationship. Every night we would argue about the cost of food and labor, menu prices, hours of operation. It was too stifling and kept me from having the freedom to act on my gut. I wanted to be able to pivot on a dime and not have to explain myself, partly because of ego and partly because I was flying by the seat of my pants, creating as I went along. I didn't know whether something would work or not. I just wanted to try it out and see. I started a *People's History* book club, an eco-feminist coffeehouse series with my friend Njoki Njehu, who worked at Greenpeace, an environmental discussion group with Joe Libertelli, a local environmentalist, and lots of other events that may not have been great at generating revenue but that I found personally fulfilling beyond financial measure.

In response to the nuclear testing that the French government undertook in the Pacific in 1996, Njoki suggested an action to bring light to this horrific environmental disaster. It was close to fall, when the new batch of Beaujolais Nouveau wine was coming to market. This wine is made from the first harvest of the season and it is the biggest day of the year for the French wine industry.

At the time, because Njoki was working for Greenpeace, she knew how to draw attention from the media by using unorthodox tactics. "Let's dump French wine at Dupont Circle and start a boycott," she suggested. This was right up my alley. The word environmental terrorism was new to me but I loved the drama of such an idea and the attention it would generate. And, of course, it connected with the business of running a restaurant. Njoki sent out a press release alerting the media to the action. A day later we gathered a group of activists and headed to the circle carrying two cases of French wines. We made a lot of noise getting there, with drums and horns to attract attention. At the fountain in the center of Dupont Circle, each person held up a bottle as Njoki and I spoke from a makeshift stage. When we were done, she took the bullhorn and shouted. "Let's dump the French. No more nukes." We emptied the bottles into the fountain. This action surely warranted a publicity-attracting arrest, but alas, there was no police presence. We ended the action shouting, "No more nukes! No more nukes!" We headed back to the restaurant where we blacked out the French wines from the wine list, adding a note on each menu explaining why they were no longer available. I began to see first-hand how a restaurant could be a force for something more powerful than just feeding people.

Two years after opening Luna Books, it was becoming obvious that I needed to part ways with my brother and father. We discussed the possibility of splitting the businesses with Café Luna on one side and Skewers and Luna Books on the other. This at first sounded feasible but we soon realized that, as all three businesses were located in the same building, they depended on one another. They shared a kitchen, a back door and staff. Somehow, we needed to come up with a more workable plan.

The next few weeks were filled with haggling over the split. Tensions were running high and patience wearing thin. In the meantime, business was beginning to suffer. Staff morale was at an all-time low. The employees sensed the strain, and we ended up losing some key people. At that point, it was becoming obvious that the only way to keep peace in the family was to disentangle the business arrangement. We agreed on a fair buyout amount, and I took the money and decided to start my own restaurant.

I decided to call the new place Luna Grill and Diner, playing off the Cafe Luna success. It was just a few blocks down from Cafe Luna, close to the business district, with thousands of office workers literally steps away. It was a turnkey restaurant that once served crepes but hadn't had much traction and went belly up fairly quickly after opening. There was little to do in the way of construction. Much of the work was cosmetic, requiring just a little paint and some minor carpentry. I asked my friend Cheryl Swanack to do a mural of moons and planets in keeping with the theme. Cheryl was a genius in collage work, using cans of spray paint with a round pizza pan, a piece of cardboard, or a string tied to a nail in the center to make a perfect circle. She hand-drew a sun with streaming golden yellow rays and the face of a woman. Her work was free-form and done without much planning, just applying layer on layer till she found something that worked. I loved watching her creative process and got many ideas that I would later use when creating the murals at Busboys and Poets.

I hired a chef, Gerry, who turned out to be an exceptional cook, especially when it came to making soups and desserts. He knew how to put the "comfort" in comfort food. His creamy chicken pot pie with homemade puff pastry, and filled with peas, carrots and large chunks of chicken, felt like a warm blanket on a cold day. His meatloaf mixed with chopped wild mushrooms and onions, then slathered with ketchup and baked to a charred sweetness was a big hit, as was the panko-coated fried chicken with beurre blanc. He marinated his chicken with buttermilk and Tabasco for an extra jolt. He made bread daily using whatever herb he had in the kitchen: dill, rosemary, basil. The whole staff waited at the pick-up line to split the first loaf out of the oven. Cracking it open, watching the steam rise and guessing what herb he had used was a real treat. No one waited for it to cool off, it was too mouthwatering.

Gerry was a genius but he was not without his demons. On most days he was easy to work with, shuffling around the kitchen in his clogs, helping out wherever he was needed. But he was intense, so tightly wound that when in a bad mood, the smallest thing would send him into a tirade and a funk that lingered for the entire day. After a particularly rough night out, his blue eyes would be bloodshot and his beard untrimmed. He would throw things against the wall when something wasn't prepped correctly and curse at the top of his lungs when a waiter mixed up an order. We knew to keep our distance on those occasions.

In today's kitchens, Gerry's bad moods would not be tolerated. Back then, kitchens and chefs were different. The chefs had *carte blanche*. They yelled, harassed, threatened, drank, and assaulted with little or no consequences. Gerry lasted about three years, far longer than I expected. But he was a handful to manage. After he left, I promised myself I would not rely on any more chefs, but rather on my line cooks, promoting them from within. After all, the most important thing in a restaurant is consistency, and line cooks are the ones who make that happen. It was a promise to myself that I would break repeatedly, always thinking that maybe, this time, things might be different.

Soon after opening Luna Grill and Diner, I sent a postcard to Phyllis Richman at the *Washington Post* inviting her to visit. This time I was less desperate for the review to be a kickstarter for the business; rather, I was looking for validation. When Phyllis showed up a few weeks after we opened, I had forgotten that I had sent the card. By then, having opened Skewers and Cafe Luna, I had intrigued her by the places I had created, and she saw me as a significant contributor to the food and restaurant scene in DC.

Just as we had when she reviewed Skewers, she and I locked eyes momentarily, and again I pretended not to recognize her and seated her at the next available space, which didn't open up for nearly 40 minutes. The lunch rush at Luna Grill and Diner lasted about 2 hours and was already intense. Tables were just inches apart and the waiting area was barely the size of a phone booth. People just hovered at the door and made you feel bad if you were sitting too long. But actually, the crush worked to our advantage. I would frequently hear comments about the place feeling "*so* New York," the Big Apple being regarded as the pinnacle of hip sophistication.

Phyllis's review was once more as good as I could have ever hoped for. She described Luna Grill and Diner as a "Diner Deluxe." I was over the moon (pun intended). She went into great detail about the quality of the food, raving about the potatoes. She wrote: "What's a diner meal without potatoes? The french fries here are soft, thick and greaseless—just wonderful. Fried sweet potatoes are plump and moist, with crunchy charred edges. But who could pass up the mashed potatoes, so rough and lumpy, with a crater of gravy? On my first visit to Luna Grill, the woman at the next table ordered a bowl of mashed potatoes for dessert. She was a woman who knows what's what. I bet she had the fries as an appetizer."

While things couldn't have been going better at Luna Grill and Diner, I missed the old gatherings of friends and activists that I'd hosted at Luna Books. So, I started to invite small groups of about a dozen or so to gather once a week at the new place for discussions around the latest political or social issues. Ralph Nader once again became a regular.

Business was by now booming. For the first time, I wasn't living paycheck to paycheck. I was even able to save. Thoughts of opening another location began to dance in my head and I called my real estate agent to start looking. Knowing that I had a hit on my hands, I decided to try to duplicate it. I opened the next Luna Grill and Diner about two years after the first one. This branch opened in an Arlington, Virginia, shopping center conveniently located halfway between DC and where I lived in Annandale. Having already learned the ins and outs of lease negotiations and other necessary business skills, I was able to oversee the entire process all the way through to the opening, dealing with contractors, plumbers, hood specialists, and wine and beer salespeople. I also met with as many community and civic groups as I could to find and made sure that by the time the place opened, there was enough buzz to get it going straight away. Sure enough, once again, success was immediate.

A year after I opened Luna Grill and Diner, Bill Clinton ordered airstrikes against Iraq. Saddam Hussein allegedly refused to give unfettered access to UN inspectors to search for weapons of mass destruction, warranting the strikes. Dozens of civilians were killed in the attack, which was meant to degrade Iraq's military capabilities. At that time, the Monica Lewinsky scandal was unfolding, and Congress was chomping at the bit to get Bill. So, confronted with a scandal, he did what many presidents have done over the centuries: he started a war. Many people, including myself, believed that this was more about weapons of mass *distraction* than destruction and I wasn't shy about saying so. Soon, word got around that an Iraqi business-man was willing to speak out about the war. Media descended on Luna Grill and Diner. I became a go-to talking head for major outlets on Iraq issues, leading to several appearances on NPR, CNN and NBC, as well as local stations. I often met journalists seeking an interview at the restaurant. It was gratify-ing to be able to express my opinion and know that what I was saying mattered. At the same time, I was nervous about the fallout that such appearances might have, for me personally and for the business, but I figured that whatever business I might lose, I would also gain from those with whom my message res-onated. One thing was for sure, being silent was not an option.

15

SHOWTIME

The first Gulf War, like all wars, was built on lies. One particularly notable doozie came from a teary-eyed daughter of the Kuwaiti ambassador. Coached by a PR firm, she fabricated a shocking story about Iraqi soldiers entering a Kuwaiti neonatal hospital, unplugging baby incubators, and tossing the premature babies onto the ground. Her story seemed plausible, given the propaganda leading up to the war. I even bought into it. As it turned out, her tears should have earned her an Oscar. The lies didn't stop there. Others included an invented story about satellite images of Iraqi troops massing on the Saudi border. The truth behind these and other lies wouldn't come to light until it was too late.

Dick Cheney was Secretary of Defense at the time and helped to orchestrate the charade, spoon-feeding the news media as though they were hungry toddlers. A decade later he would become Vice President to the younger Bush, with a new set of lies and deceptions for a second Gulf War that created far more devastation and destruction than the first one.

Once again, the media played a significant role in promoting the war. CNN's wall-to-wall coverage was exhausting to watch and gave little in the way of analysis or impartiality. And once again experts sprouted up from the woodwork: Richard Perle, a.k.a. The Prince of Darkness, Henry Kissinger, once fittingly called the minion of Satan, and William Kristol led the chorus behind Dick Cheney, the Darth Vader Secretary of Defense. We watched live reports from Bernard Shaw in Baghdad, cheerleading the military assault, at first from the balcony of the Al-Rashid Hotel and then, as the bombs began to rain, from under his desk inside. "The skies over Baghdad have been illuminated," he declared. This continued for days on end. My only lifeline to sanity was commiserating with Iraqi friends. The idea that Americans were learning Iraqi history and culture through this warped lens of war didn't sit well with any of us. Iraq, the cradle of civilization, was reduced to Saddam Hussein. We needed to do something. And rather than sulk, we went into action.

A group of about a dozen Iraqis met nightly in each other's living rooms. We chatted for hours while CNN played in the background. We consoled one another, drank gallons of dark tea and sent out for pizza. We talked. We laughed. We even cried. It was much-needed therapy. Each night brought new ideas and new energy. We wanted to enter the hearts of Americans, and we figured that culture was the path to do so. Culture peels away the calcified crust of social constructs and brings light to our humanity. Americans needed to learn about Iraq, to put a human face on the grotesque spectacle being presented on television, to learn that Iraq is the land where the Tigris and Euphrates meet, the land of Babylon and Hammurabi, of artists and poets and the tales of One Thousand and One Nights.

In less than a month, the Mesopotamia Cultural Society was born. We debated for hours about the name. We were split on Mesopotamia vs Iraq. In the end, despite my protests, Mesopotamia won. The majority of the group felt that using Iraq's ancient name would open up more doors. It would be an easier sell to members of Congress and others who could affect the necessary foreign policy change we were seeking. Having secured a 501(c)3 status, MCS was ready to launch.

It was an easy sell. The culture of Mesopotamia resonated with Americans, although, as I'd anticipated, many didn't connect Mesopotamia with Iraq. Even Iraqis in the diaspora wanted to know more about their own history and culture. When we put out the word, calling all Iraqi artists, poets, writers and whomever to get in touch, we had no idea who would turn up. Within days, dozens of people were contacting us. They were from all over the world, as far away as China. They included Iraqi artists who had been exiled for decades; calligraphers, printmakers, ceramic artists; well-known figures such as Mohammed Al Saqqar and Diah Azzawi.

Several galleries opened their doors to us. But our mission wasn't only to showcase Iraqi art and artists in galleries. We were looking to impact US policy toward Iraq. We wanted diplomacy and level-headedness, not bravado and aggression. We knew that US policy in the Middle East was lopsided. Our work was cut out for us.

We went to Congress and visited our representatives. Jim Moran, the congressman from Arlington, Virginia, was particularly helpful and forthcoming. It didn't hurt that his chief of staff was of Lebanese ancestry. Moran had been deeply involved in Middle East politics for years. His support for Palestinian human rights would later cost him his seat in Congress. We met with his staff several times and convinced the congressman to sponsor an exhibit of Iraqi art at the Cannon House Office Building, where his office was located. The entrance to the building faces the Capitol and features a huge rotunda that everyone going in, congressmen, staffers, lobbyists and ordinary citizens, must pass through. It was the first time such an exhibit would be shown at such a prominent site. Thousands of people would finally have an opportunity to see Iraq in a different light. It was a real coup to have this venue for our first exhibit.

We wanted to make sure that the exhibit was perfectly curated and displayed. We used our own funds to obtain professional framing. Nizar Jawdat, an Iraqi architect turned gallery owner who lived in Washington, DC, was brought in to help along with his wife, Ellen. They later became close friends and advisors to us.

We invited House members and their staff to the opening of the show. Jim Moran came along, and a handful of other congressmen made an appearance. We were delighted to have achieved such a prominent presence in such a short time. The day following the exhibit, the *Washington Times,* a right-wing newspaper owned by the Moonies, ran a front-page hatchet job about the exhibit accusing Jim Moran of providing comfort to the enemy. Fortunately, it didn't get much traction; in fact, we used the article to do a fundraiser for Jim soon thereafter, raising tens of thousands of dollars for his campaign.

Our next exhibit came just days later during the Convention of the Arab American Anti-Discrimination Committee (ADC), one of the largest gatherings of Arab Americans in the country. MCS became the talk of the convention. Hundreds of people enjoyed the exhibit, praising it and offering assistance. Others were not so supportive. Some visitors, in particular those with interests in Iraqi business opportunities and ties to American neo-liberals like Paul Wolfowitz and Donald Rumsfeld, accused MCS of being apologists for Saddam Hussein. It was a familiar line of attack and meant that every time MCS issued a statement it had to be preceded by a vigorous denunciation of the Iraqi leader, up to and including comparing him to Hitler. Only then could any reasonable discussion commence. It was wearying but had to be done.

Despite the critics, I saw through MCS how a small group of people could truly make a difference. It wasn't easy, it was all-consuming. But in the end it was worth it. We were making a difference, albeit a small one.

With the Gulf War behind us, I started thinking of new ventures that would allow me to incorporate my activism and attract people who believed in a more peaceful world. I missed having a bookstore, all the events that centered around it, and the community it created. Soon after I left, Luna Books and Democracy Center ceased offering book events and the space became little more than an overflow for Skewers and a place to host an occasional birthday or private dinner.

I looked for a suitable location to open a new place in the vicinity of Dupont Circle. I needed somewhere close to Luna Grill and Diner that I could get to easily. At the base of a Marriott Residence Inn was an empty shell. It was the right size, about 5,000 square feet, and had a good street presence with large windows overlooking P Street. I had driven by it a few times and noticed the "For Lease" sign. It was directly opposite a spot that used to be occupied by a restaurant called Herb's. The owner, Herb White, was a beloved and well-connected DC native, a patron of the arts and founder of The DC Arts Center. A tall, handsome man with soft features and steely blue eyes, he once had a part as a stand-in for Peter O'Toole in Lawrence of Arabia. Herb's was the place where Washingtonians were able to get a taste of Hollywood. It held fundraisers for theaters and art organizations, making Herb the darling of the arts community in DC. The place was open late at night and frequently had a group of cast members whooping it up around a grand piano during the post-show party. It was rowdy, loud, colorful and it served decent bistro fare: steak frites, hamburgers and grilled fish. Its closure left a void for years in the DC restaurant scene. Being an artist myself, I loved Herb's and wanted to bring a little bit of LA and NYC to DC. I also wanted to surround myself with artists and creatives. The dreamers and change makers, and those who make the world more livable.

A couple of weeks earlier I had attended a performance of *La Bohème* at the Kennedy Center. It reminded me of when I'd seen the musical *Rent*, a modern version of *La Bohème*, on Broadway. I loved both performances and particularly the lead, Mimi, a wonderfully rich character, unapologetic and sexy and with a love for life despite many flaws and obstacles. When she dies at the end, of tuberculosis in the Puccini opera and of AIDS in the Broadway show, everyone cries. I decided to name the restaurant after her. I envisaged creating a place that would attract artists, theatergoers and people who appreciate culture. It would have a bohemian yet upscale feel; a bit of Moulin Rouge with deep warm colors, a carpet with a big floral design and thick curtains with gold tassels. I splurged on a Yamaha grand piano and placed it prominently in the center of the room. I wanted the wait staff to be like the patrons: artists, poets, and singers. I put an ad in the local theater rag. I hired an artistic director, Brian, who was a gifted pianist. He never used sheet music and played by ear. All you had to do was hum a bar or two for him and he'd run with it. He took the first crack at the applicants, making sure they made the cut talent-wise. Only after he OK'd them did I interview them for the job. Talent was a prerequisite, serving experience was not.

Brian and I met for hours discussing the type of music I was looking for and the ability of the applicants to perform it. I was aware that DC does not have the depth of theater talent of New York, so we relied on music schools. We had a constant pipeline from Catholic and Howard Universities with some great musical theater and jazz singers. Every server had two one-hour sessions with Brian for rehearsal each week. They also had to come early for their shift and brush up on their repertoire for the evening. On any given night, Mimi's had four or five servers taking care of tables and belting out tunes from shows like *Les Misérables, Phantom of the Opera, A Chorus Line, Rent*, even *The Rocky Horror Picture Show*. There were group songs, during which the entire staff would break away from service and sing.

The guests ate it up. They loved cheering their server as they stood by the piano, backed up by Brian, singing their hearts out. There were a handful of real stars, each with their own specialty. David, with curly copper hair and a tall, buff frame, wearing the tightest possible jeans, chaps, spurs and a cowboy hat, did a rousing version of "Oklahoma!" By the time he got to spelling out O-K-L-A-H-O-M-A, the crowd was on its feet, stomping and cheering and throwing money at him. It never failed. Then there was Madeline, a sultry, willowy blond who did an amazing rendition of Carole King's "Natural Woman." By the time she neared the end, she had the entire place singing. Even the men were feeling like a "natural woman." And there was Donna, the hostess, a short, Black woman with deep dimples, who did "Tenderly" so beautifully that it brought tears each time I heard it. People would wait to be seated until she finished her set. She would have menus in one hand and a wireless microphone in the other, singing while seating customers.

New Year's Eve at Mimi's was off the charts. It was sold out weeks in advance. I would get phone calls begging for a last-minute table. As the date came closer, I stopped answering my phone knowing that we couldn't accept one more reservation, no matter who it was. I was on a roll. Success was following me everywhere I went. It seemed I knew what made a great restaurant and what got people in the door. Now I had three different establishments close to one another, all doing better than I could have imagined and receiving raves from customers and critics. Along the way, I was honing my vision: using food as a lure to get people in the door and then giving them something else. But what else should that something be? Being around artists and musicians was exciting and energizing, but Mimi's did not lend itself to the kind of political gatherings that I craved.

With three locations under my belt, I found myself spending almost every waking hour at one of them, splitting my time between Mimi's and Luna Grill. I loved engaging with regulars and spending hours discussing politics. It gave me comfort to see how many people were on "my side," and some of them later became close friends.

Mimi Conway was one of those people with whom I made an instant connection. She lived a few blocks away from Mimi's and became a regular, dining at least twice a week, sometimes bringing friends to introduce them to me and to the place. She had the most disarming personality. I never saw Mimi angry or in any way less than charming. She wore the most outrageous cat eyeglasses with psychedelic frames that matched her outfits.

"This is my dear friend, Andy Shallal. He's an extraordinary Iraqi peace activist and a gifted artist," she would say with a wide smile while introducing me to others. She and I would spend many afternoons sharing a plate of hummus and a pot of green tea discussing everything and anything: The Patriot Act. The war on terrorism. Cheney. Saddam. Art. Culture. I loved talking to Mimi; she was worldly and well informed, and a great listener. She was one of the people I felt I could turn to during those times when I was feeling isolated.

"I think you have a kindred spirit in the artistic director at Theater J," Mimi told me on one of those extended afternoon get-togethers. I had no idea what Theater J was. "I want to introduce you to him. His name is Ari Roth. He's a terrific person and I know you will adore him. Maybe the two of you can do something together. You know, collaborate on something extraordinary," she said.

"The J," as it was colloquially known, was the theater at the Jewish Community Center (JCC) in DC. Mimi happened to be a board member there. Ari was in the middle of producing a festival dealing with Israel and Palestine. He called it New Voices of the Middle East. "I think he can use your expertise on the subject," Mimi told me. She saw her role as the neutral bridge since she "didn't have a dog in the fight," as she would say. Of course, there are more dogs in that fight than a Westminster Dog Show and each one has their own geo-political or religious agenda. There are no innocent bystanders when it comes to Israel and Palestine and I had my doubts about a festival coming out of the JCC. Nonetheless, I wanted to keep an open mind and see what Ari had to say.

One afternoon Mimi and I walked over to the JCC to meet Ari. It was located on 16th Street in a building with an imposing white marble edifice featuring tall columns and a grand stadium-sized staircase that emptied onto the sidewalk. A big banner hung across the facade advertising upcoming shows. The main entrance was on the side of the building, and in front of it a stern-looking uniformed police officer paced back and forth. He kept a close watch of who came and went, and I felt particularly scrutinized. This wasn't like other community centers, where doors are left open for anyone to enter. Here you had to be ID'd and buzzed in. Mimi was a familiar face and well-known by the guards. When the cop realized I was with her, his demeanor changed, and he became all smiles.

It was the first time I had set foot inside a JCC. Behind the marble floor lobby was a kosher restaurant and downstairs was a swimming pool and gym, a day-care center, a library, as well as administrative offices. The theater took up most of the second floor. It was a community center in all senses of the word. In the past, whenever I had walked by, I often wondered what happened behind those walls. I guessed, however, that I would not feel welcome.

We sat at a table in the restaurant, which was nothing fancy. It had a dozen or so cloth-covered tables that spilled into the lobby. A wide staircase with an ornate wrought-iron railing led to the second floor where the theater was located. Inside it was a beehive of activity. People in jogging outfits; parents with children in tow; little girls with ballet tutus. I had no idea what Ari looked like but tried to pick him out from the crowd. Moments later he appeared, looking like an artistic director out of Central Casting: Upper 40s, tousled hair, thinning but devoid of gray and matching bushy eyebrows, above a wide smile. He held a leather-bound notebook under his arm and walked with the balls of his feet first, giving him a slight forward tilt. His light blue button-down shirt with rolled sleeves was halfway untucked. He immediately extended his arms to Mimi; they hugged and kissed on one cheek.

"This is my dear friend Andy Shallal, he's Iraqi and he owns Mimi's," she said cheerfully, gesturing towards me as if she was presenting a prize winner.

We shook hands. His handshake wasn't as firm as I expected, and I quickly adjusted the firmness of my grip to match his.

"I've heard so much about you. Mimi should be your PR agent," I said, while continuing to shake his hand slowly.

Ari laughed.

"Mimi herself is extraordinary," he said, adding, "We are lucky to have such an accomplished individual on our board."

We chatted a bit about the weather and our families, trying to get the measure of each other.

"So tell me about Theater J," I asked.

Ari opened up into a monologue about his plans for the festival. Beyond that point, I hardly said a word. I just nodded and listened. Once in a while my mind would wander. What would my mother think if she saw me here? Would she be upset, ashamed, surprised? At home, in her eyes, European Jews were seen as the enemy. They were Zionists and hated Arabs. American Jews, unlike the ones she knew in Iraq, were not to be trusted.

My mother would tell a story about a local Jewish jeweler who knew her mother and would bring a handful of diamonds and jewelry to show her. He would leave the entire stash for her to try out at home. He would return days later to see if she liked anything and would often walk away without a sale thanking her. My mother would say, "Those Jews know how to do business. They are so clever. Not like us." Things changed dramatically in 1948, when the Nakba occurred. Jews migrated in droves to establish the state of Israel, my mother's neighbors among them. I decided that, for now, I would keep this meeting at the JCC to myself and not tell my parents.

I also remembered the stories my father told me about Jews during his childhood back in Iraq, in Baghdad, when things were different. My father had fond memories of his Jewish neighbors. He grew up with Jewish friends. He would earn extra coins as a "goy boy," lighting fires for cooking and running errands for the neighbors on the Jewish Sabbath. But that was a long time ago, before the Nakba.

During our chat Ari mentioned that he was doing a play dealing with Israelis and Palestinians as part of his Middle East festival. It was a one-act monologue written by David Hare, a British playwright who visited the region in 1997 and witnessed first-hand life for the Palestinians under occupation. He named it *Via Dolorosa* (The Way of Suffering) after the path that Jesus took carrying the cross on his walk to be crucified.

He chronicled the conditions he witnessed during his trip using the voices of 33 different people, both Palestinians and Israelis, from government as well as civil society. It was a delicately crafted piece that allowed both sides to be heard. Ari, however, knew his audience and was worried that his mostly older Jewish patrons might feel that it gave too much weight to the Palestinian side of the story. He was particularly concerned about longtime JCC members who were generally more conservative, and who tended to be the biggest donors. Much to his credit, though, Ari wanted to use theater as an entryway into the hearts and minds of the audience. "I refuse to do *Fiddler on The Roof*," he told me. "I want provocative plays that get people thinking. I have nothing against Jerry Bock or Sheldon Harnick or Neil Simon, but I want to do plays that matter."

Of course, he also wanted to fill his 200-seat theater and in a city with nearly 100 professional theaters, he was looking for a niche. As an Arab, I saw it as an opportunity to do something meaningful as well. Ari was providing a platform to showcase a viewpoint that few of his patrons ever got to see or hear. An Arab perspective about the Israeli-Palestinian conflict was not something a typical JCC would offer. Ari had been thinking about this and wanted to host dialogues at the end of each night the play was running. The post-theater conversations would be a way to allay his worries about being accused of bias. He wanted to have me there to deflect any criticism, acting as his shield against any arrows that might come his way.

Ari and I met several times after our initial get-together. We were often worlds apart in our political views on Israel and Palestine, but we remained friends over the years. We knew when to push and when to back off, keeping a cordial distance when it came to sensitive topics such as the Boycott Divestment Sanctions (BDS)

movement, which I saw as an effective non-violent campaign to end the occupation, and which, I suspected, he saw as discriminatory and anti-Semitic. There were many other points of disagreement, including the right of return for Palestinians and the use of the word "apartheid" or "settler colonialism" when discussing Israel. Ari wanted to provoke without offending. He had the JCC board to answer to while I was a free agent. But despite these issues, I was excited to see where the project would lead.

On opening night, I arrived at the theater early and helped to set up tables in the lobby to create what became known as the Peace Café. Along with the menu of ideas, we placed several candles on each table to create a nice vibe and a bowl of hummus with Palestinian olive oil and large loaves of pita bread to share. We also had a tray of dates that we passed around. As people filed in, I stood at the entrance to the theater along with Ari and Mimi and welcomed the crowd. I was a bundle of nerves, uncertain about what to expect and the evident pitfalls we faced. Soon every seat was taken. The air crackled with opening night excitement. We took our seats in the front row. The lights dimmed and Ari got up on stage. "Welcome to opening night of *Via Dolorosa*," he said. Before he finished his sentence, the crowd broke out in a vigorous applause. "I would like to bring up two special guests to the stage. My partners in crime, Andy Shallal and Mimi Conway," Mimi and I joined him. "For the past few weeks the three of us have been working on something very special and, we believe, much needed. A venue for dialogue between Jews, Arabs, Muslims and others who believe in peace in the Middle East." More fervent applause. "We hope you can join us after the play in the lobby for this important conversation."

With that we all returned to our seats, the lights went to a full blackout and then to a spot on a lone stool in the middle of the stage from which David Jackson, the actor who was playing David Hare, addressed the audience. The monologue lasted nearly 90 minutes, meandering through the West Bank, Tel Aviv and a refugee camp. There were several dozen characters from all sides of the conflict representing almost every viewpoint. Politicians, artists, writers, journalists, refugees, exiles. There were words coming out of David Jackson's mouth that were uttered for the first time on the JCC stage. Words like "intifada," "Nakba" and "apartheid," and phrases like "right of return."

The play ended with an enthusiastic standing ovation. Almost everyone made their way to the lobby afterwards for the Peace Café. Extra chairs had to be dragged in from a nearby storage closet to accommodate the overflow. Everyone was instructed to share the food that was on their table. We intentionally kept the bread whole to encourage tearing it and passing it to the next person. To kickstart the dialogue on the right foot, we pulled lines from the play as a "menu of ideas" resembling a restaurant menu, maintaining the café metaphor. For extra measure I had reached out to George Mason University School for Conflict Analysis and Resolution and asked for graduate student volunteers to help facilitate the dialogue. We tried to cover all bases to avoid anything going wrong. And it worked! The first Peace Cafés were a huge success. On subsequent nights people often lingered way past the allotted time, only to be kicked out by the custodial staff of the JCC. Many came on more than one night. This continued during the entire three-week run of *Via Dolorosa* at Theater J.

Once the play ended, the Peace Café moved out of the JCC and transferred to Mimi's. Unlike at the Center, at Mimi's, I had no one to answer to. I didn't have donors to appease or a board to approve what I did or didn't do. There, I was free to invite Palestinian activists working on a variety of campaigns like right of return, ending the occupation, or a one-state solution, issues that were too controversial for the JCC. Soon a core of Peace Café attendees was formed. They were a mix of Arabs and Jews and others too. Mimi's Peace Cafés became part of the itinerary for peace activists coming through town. At one point I was hosting weekly events on Sunday mornings that consistently attracted a few dozen participants, along with some of the top political and cultural figures of the region. People like Issa Amro, Ali Abu Awad, Hanan Ashrawi and many others. We also hosted authors such as Norman Finkelstein and the late Edward Said. Subsequently I started a Peace Café book club, which held readings of books such as *Arab and Jew* by David Shipler, the *New York Times* Jerusalem Bureau Chief in the 1980s. David himself attended several times to join the conversation.

One Sunday morning we hosted a Peace Café with Diana Bhutu, the Palestinian-Canadian PLO legal advisor who was in town for a conference. The conversation lingered into brunch time. While the first brunch guests were arriving, Diana was making her closing remarks touching on Palestinian liberation, self-determination and the Israeli occupation. The first three brunch customers who came in looked familiar. I realized it was Charles Krauthammer, the neocon *Washington Post* columnist, Bill Kristol, editor of *The Weekly Standard*, and George Will, the libertarian political commentator. They had just finished their Sunday morning program on TV, a show which in my view severely distorted the Israel–Palestine issue, spewing misinformation and disinformation every Sunday before millions of viewers. They certainly didn't expect to be in the middle of a Palestinian/Israeli debate at a brunch spot. They looked perturbed, as if they'd just been ambushed. They ate quickly and left. It was the last time I saw them.

As the months went by, I noticed a dwindling number of Palestinian and Arab participants at the Peace Cafés. Mouna, a Palestinian woman who had been a diehard regular, suddenly stopped attending. I called her to find out what happened.

"Anas, I have to tell you, I've been doing these dialogues with Jews for a long time. I am tired. I always feel used. Drained. I am not willing to be a therapist for Jewish liberals. I just can't do it anymore," she said. In the end, I couldn't either. I told Ari, "Listen, I think the most important conversation needs to be within the Jewish community. They need to acknowledge that the conflict is not about Arabs and Jews eating at a café in Washington, DC, but rather about an ongoing brutal occupation that has gone on for far too long. Arabs and Jews have gotten along just fine for centuries. If we continue to think of this conflict as one between two equals, we'll never reach an understanding or a way forward."

16

RUBBLE AND RHETORIC

It took the news a while to settle in. My thoughts were fresh
from the Y2K scare just a little over a year before. The idea of
planes crashing into a skyscraper didn't seem so far-fetched. It
was most likely a computer error. But then the second plane,
and then the Pentagon. Suddenly it was all too real: America
was under attack. 9/11 unleashed a cascade of emotions. On
that day, I had never felt so American and yet so un-American.
The men on that plane had names that were familiar to me.
They looked like my family. They were Muslim men like me.
And despite the horrific crime they committed, I could understand what might have driven them to it and I felt guilty as
hell for having those thoughts. The rest of the day was mostly
a blur.

At Dupont Circle the streets quickly turned into parking
lots. Nothing was moving. The air was thick with fear and frustration. Sidewalks were full of people rushing around seemingly
directionless. Some were looking up into the clear morning sky,
as if summoning a higher power or trying to spot a plane or a
missile. Businesses were quick to close. It was as if the end of
the world was near.

Mimi's and both Luna Grills were brimming with people
glued to the television sets above the bars. By the time I got to
Luna Grill, my first stop, the staff was already overwhelmed by

the jittery crowd. Most just wanted coffee or a place to huddle and feel safe. The restaurants had become known as community gathering places and served that purpose well. By noon, three hours after the attacks, we were the only businesses within blocks that hadn't closed shop. For me, closing at that point stopped being an option. We needed to stay open. And for the next few hours people kept trickling in and out, while the kitchen continued to serve sandwiches and other refreshments and place them on the bar for anyone to help themselves free of charge.

Around midday, I received a phone call from *Washington Post* columnist Courtland Milloy. I knew him from the Cafe Luna days during the first Gulf War and I trusted his reporting and viewpoint. By then it was determined that the perpetrators were Arab men. He asked me how I was doing, if everything was OK. He wanted to stop by and chat a bit. When he arrived an hour later, the place was still packed. We sat in a corner booth and spoke for well over an hour. He wanted to know how I felt. What it was like for someone who was Muslim and Arab, living in America at that moment. What was going through my mind? What did I think the response should be?

His article was published in the Metro section a few days later, detailing the anguish that Arabs and Muslims were facing, having their loyalty questioned, being held responsible for what happened on 9/11, and having to condemn the attacks over and over again for fear of being perceived as sympathizers. It was an honest, empathetic, humanistic piece.

It was well after 11 p.m. when we finally closed. By then the streets had cleared. Armored vehicles patrolled every corner. Men in camouflage stood at each intersection, large machine guns across their chests, fingers on the trigger. It was reminiscent of a revolution back in Iraq, but a lot more orderly.

On the way home, as I crossed the 14th Street Bridge, I noticed that the air smelled of charred debris, like burning paper. A few hundred yards away, I could see the Pentagon. It was glowing with spotlights pointing at the gaping hole where the plane had hit just hours earlier. Dozens of workers were sifting through the rubble. Fire trucks surrounded the building, smoke was still rising in the bright haze, white specs still floating in the balmy summer air. There were few cars on I-395. I made sure to stay in the slow lane and not exceed the speed limit.

By the time I got home it was close to midnight. Turning into my street, every one of the eleven homes on Chapelwood Court except ours had a stars and stripes flag hanging on a post. It looked like a parade route. Marjan had warned me about the flags when we spoke on the phone earlier that evening. "There are flags everywhere!" she said, evidently alarmed. "I went looking and couldn't find one," she added. "I went to K-Mart. They were all sold out! I even went to several gas stations."

Chapelwood Court was one of many new developments in Fairfax County, Virginia, part of a seemingly endless building boom in the 1990s. Practically every other household was a military family. Talk about using civilians as human shields. The rest was a mix of professionals from various countries. Most of them had moved in within a couple of months of one another. And in due time we all knew each other by name. Our kids attended the same schools. There were no fences between the houses. Lawns were weed-free and kept to below four inches. No one had to enforce the rules. Peer pressure did the job.

By the next day, the anxiety from the day before had begun to melt into sadness. The kind of sadness that is hard to pinpoint and hard to shake off. Neighbors were out in the center of the cul-de-sac, talking, shaking their heads, arms folded. Marjan and I came out and joined the group of a dozen or so.

Among them were the other "foreigners" who had moved into the neighborhood: the Mahdis. Originally from Iran, Reza and Neda Mahdi had moved in shortly after us. They traveled all the time and mostly kept to themselves when home, so we hardly saw them. As we joined the group they peeled off and went back to their house.

Now just Marjan and I were left to explain a different perspective on things to our white neighbors. Before we could say anything, we would have to prove our patriotism to the rest of the group. Our condemnation of the attacks needed to be more emphatic than anyone else's. Our arms had to be more tightly folded; our head shakes more vigorous. I dreaded the encounter and as expected the floodgates of racist garbage came pouring out like water through a breached dam.

"Who would do such a thing?" my next-door neighbor Joe turned to me, getting right in my face with what felt like an accusing manner. Joe was a military man, a retired colonel. He loved to gossip and was very opinionated, engaging me in conversation whenever he could. I never trusted him with anything that he might use against me. "What have we done to deserve this?" he demanded, his outrage barely beneath the surface. He barreled on, adding expletives to talk of settling scores, of obliterating the enemy, of nuking them. His fulminations carried more than a hint of racism.

Karen, another neighbor, turned to Marjan, her eyes welling with tears. "Do you need a flag, I noticed you don't have one?" she blurted out through sniffles. "No, we're good," I responded quickly and politely, hoping she'd move on. "We have an extra one?" she added, not letting it drop. "I'm not into flags," I said, still maintaining a decorum. "I don't think they're necessary. Flags are divisive and I'd rather not have one." I could feel the steam rising from my head.

As the conversation began to devolve into a Fox News version of geopolitics, I excused myself and went inside the house. I was afraid that I would say too much and be perceived as a sympathizer or worse. For the first time since coming to America, I began to worry for my family's safety and gave serious thought to leaving. But where would we go? I had no idea.

An hour later, Marjan called me over to the window. "Look," she said pointing to the mailbox. Someone had planted a small American flag on it. I was angry and hurt. It was as if someone placed a burning cross on my lawn. I felt violated, foreign, unwelcome. I wanted to march over with the flag to Joe's and Karen's, those most likely to have planted it there, and give them a piece of my mind. But I opted instead to lay low. I removed the flag and brought it inside the house.

The next day, our neighbor Robby, Karen's son and my daughter's classmate who led the Young Republicans Club at school, was seen with his friends patrolling the neighborhood with a painted sign on the back car window saying, "Arabs go home."

In the weeks and months that followed, the international situation worsened. The Bush administration launched its Global War on Terror with the invasion of Afghanistan, which became a hell on earth. I turned to the internet to find a community of like-minded people, people who did not see 9/11 as an invitation for endless war, but rather a moment of reckoning for American hegemony. I remember reading the poetry of Suheir Hammad, the Black Palestinian poet. Her words in the immediate wake of 9/11 made me realize I was not alone.

there have been no words.
i have not written one word.
no poetry in the ashes south of canal street.
no prose in the refrigerated trucks driving debris and DNA.
not one word ...

there is life here. anyone reading this is breathing, maybe
      hurting,
but breathing for sure. and if there is any light to come, it will
shine from the eyes of those who look for peace and justice
      after the
rubble and rhetoric are cleared and the phoenix has risen.

affirm life.
affirm life.
we got to carry each other now.
you are either with life, or against it.
affirm life.

These words warmed my heart and brought a much-needed
smile to my face. Despite the horror, 9/11 made it possible for
so many Arabs and Muslims to find our voice. To affirm life.
To reject the "us" against "them" set up. Being invisible was no
longer an option. 9/11 made me realize how precarious living
in America could be. As an immigrant, a Muslim and a person
of color, I once again felt vulnerable, an outsider. Once again,
I felt less American. And once again, it was an opportunity to
test American democracy and help to strengthen it.

Today when people tell me to go back to where I came
from, I laugh. I tell them, "Rather than admonishing me to
go back to where I came from, which, by the way, is not a
good option for me right now, since we destroyed that country … you should thank me each and every day for preserv-
ing whatever democracy we have. Without people of color—
Black and brown people—this country would be a bastion of
fascism. We—the people of color—are the ones who must
uphold what's left of this democracy. We are the canaries in
the coal mine and are able to sense the first whiffs of fascism.
You're welcome."

Langston Hughes said it best in his poem: "Let America be America Again." The poem ends with a call to action.

> Out of the rack and ruin of our gangster death,
> The rape and rot of graft, and stealth, and lies,
> We, the people, must redeem
> The land, the mines, the plants, the rivers.
> The mountains and the endless plain—
> All, all the stretch of these great green states—
> And make America again!

March 20, 2003, ended up being the worst birthday that I can remember. It was the day we invaded Iraq. I sat alone in front of my TV watching the bombs rain down on Baghdad, the city where I grew up. "Those motherfuckers," I yelled at the screen. "They really did it!" I'd been holding out against all odds. Maybe, just maybe, I thought, the protests and demonstrations and letter writing would have an impact. But now, sitting in my living room thousands of miles away, I watched. Buildings were reduced to dust in a split second, shooting stars kaboomed across an inky black sky streaked with night-vision green. Live reports from embedded CNN reporters were coming out in real time. "This is the shock and awe we were promised," the reporter announced enthusiastically. Words so disconnected, so cold. They made me shudder.

Americans were about to learn Iraq's geography. Fallujah. Karbala. Mosul. Basra. My family had visited these cities and towns. They were familiar to me. I knew them as places with a rich culture and a history that stretched back to before Biblical times. They were part of a land with 500 varieties of dates. We had ten varieties in our backyard alone in Baghdad where I grew up. So much that I took for granted. There are more ancient artifacts per square foot in Iraq than in any other place on the planet. This is the land of Hammurabi and the Tower of Babel and the Arch of Ctesiphon, under which my family used to picnic.

Now these places were being destroyed, their names mispronounced by a twisted American tongue that made them feel unfamiliar. Now they were being identified solely as sites of battles and massacres, torture prisons, mass graves. I was angry. Sad. Confused. And feeling desperately alone. I am Arab, a Muslim, an Iraqi. But I am also an American and this felt more like a contradiction every day that passed. The word "alien" began to haunt me.

I had seen the build-up to the war on CNN, using the same playbook from the first Gulf War. The charade of hyping up Iraq's military. I read article after article telling stories of secret caves and hidden silos of munitions and secret stashes of weapons of mass destruction. I even read about a moat with sharks around one of Saddam's mansions. I sat with friends in my living room watching Colin Powell, the Secretary of State, address the United Nations. He held up a thimble-sized vial representing one that contained deadly microbes and showed a PowerPoint featuring a cartoon truck carrying large drums full of unknown scary chemicals. "My colleagues, every statement I make today is backed up by sources, solid sources," he said. "These are not assertions. What we're giving you are facts and conclusions based on solid intelligence." It was everything I could do to keep from throwing a shoe at the television. A few years later when it was safe for him to do so, he retracted the whole story, telling the world he was duped by the CIA.

Days before I had joined the hundreds of thousands who took to the streets in protest at what was happening. My voice became hoarse from the shouting. I wanted to believe that my chanting would echo along with that of others from all over the world to bring a halt to the war. And for a moment it seemed possible. We were pushing for diplomacy, keeping the UN inspectors in Iraq to let them finish their job.

As the missiles thundered across the sky of Baghdad, I realized I had a readymade community to turn to for solidarity and comfort. That first night of the war, we called an emergency gathering at Mimi's. Within a matter of hours, more than a hundred people had showed up. The place was packed with activists and friends who wanted to do something. Anything. Despite the war raging, the gathering quickly took on a boisterous and joyful air. We ate and drank and sang songs at the piano. My sadness quickly turned to resolve. By the end of the night I felt a sense of purpose. In times like these, I learned, joy is necessary to keep going. It is easy to go into a funk and retreat. People become activists for many reasons, not the least of which is to find a tribe of like-minded folks. That night we needed each other. A shoulder to lean on or to cry on. It was much-needed self-care. Trying to make an impact and going at it alone can be overwhelming and I have seen more than a few get crushed. They gave up and walked away. I began to understand fully the secret Howard Zinn had let me in on a decade earlier about looking for small wins to propel you forward. That night at Mimi's I realized that having a readymade place for the community to gather was also an essential part for sustaining a movement.

17

BLACK BROADWAY

Despite the disasters overtaking the world, or perhaps in part because of them, Mimi's and Luna Grill were flourishing. They both served a great purpose by bringing people together. But often that was just incidental, their primary purpose was to serve food. They were, after all, restaurants, not meeting places. One, with singing servers, didn't lend itself easily to speakers and discussions. Meetings cut into the dinner hour. Tablecloths got in the way. The lighting was dim and romantic. The sound didn't carry well. The other was just a small diner with limited capacity.

I wanted to create something that was more intentionally designed for large gatherings, somewhere unabashedly progressive, a place for people to get informed, enlightened, to intersect and find their tribes. I wasn't sure I could make such a place work, however. My other businesses had all started as places to eat and had only become political hubs later. This time I wanted to begin with the end in mind. Politics and activism would be front and center. I was willing to risk everything to make it happen. I was especially keen that whatever I created would be built to attract brown and Black people. People who didn't have the luxury of being neutral on a moving train. I was sure that others would follow. As the old adage goes: build it and they will come.

After some investigation I resolved that the ideal spot for such a place would be somewhere in the U Street Corridor with a visible street presence and large storefront windows. It had to be big enough to accommodate an event with Howard Zinn, Angela Davis or Alice Walker. I knew that most landlords would scoff at such a place. So, when approaching them I would leave out the activism and politics part of my business plan. I didn't want these things to get in the way of securing a good lease. Most landlords just want their rent paid on time and without any hassles.

"Do you have a business plan and a pro forma to show me," my broker asked.

I had an idea what he was talking about, but I had never had to come up with one. Nonetheless I played along, answering affirmatively. It took me a couple days to come up with a pro forma and business plan. In it I included some of the elements necessary for the concept. A restaurant that served café fare. It would feature an espresso machine, a bar, a bookstore and a lounge area for hanging out. It would host weekly poetry programs and author events. I included the approximate number of seats and the amount of revenue I hoped to generate. I also included a ballpark amount of expenses making sure that what I planned on taking in was more than what I intended to spend.

When I presented this to the loan officer at Bank of America, he was unimpressed. My flimsy plan didn't add up. The pro forma didn't jibe with the amount of loan I was asking for. Furthermore, there was no faux leather binder, or color photos and renderings, not even a PowerPoint deck. I was turned down with a standard official form letter. I next went to Riggs Bank, the one my father had used since we came to America. They too rejected me with a single-spaced, generic letter. Next was a visit to a local bank. Once

again, a quick rejection. In the end I was turned down by five sep-
arate places. Clearly I needed a different approach. I had a good
credit score. I owned my home. I was an adult who paid his bills
on time, and I had extensive experience in business.

It was my broker who suggested to me that I try Industrial
Bank. It was a local bank, located prominently on U Street,
where it had been serving the community for over 80 years. It
is the oldest Black-owned bank in the country and it made a
point of loaning money to riskier clients, often people of color.
William Whitehead, the loan officer, sat behind an old desk
on the second floor. His starched white shirt and silk tie gave
him an air of authority. He wore a gold watch and a large gold
Howard University college ring. His hair was cut close to his
scalp and perfectly trimmed, creating a sharp outline against
his brown skin. He looked over the papers and said he would
review them and get back to me. He didn't sneer or ask too
many questions like the others.

Two days later, he called.

"I see you need $3 million but your pro forma doesn't quite
work for the amount you're asking, You're not showing enough
revenue. The numbers don't add up," he said matter-of-factly.

"What should I do?" I asked.

"Can you come by my office?"

I jumped in my car and within an hour I was sitting face to
face with him once again.

"We need to change the numbers to make them work! The
underwriter will be looking for more revenue to repay the loan
you're asking for," he said. The amount that each seat would
bring or the number of customers that would enter the door
was anyone's guess. For the next few minutes, Mr. Whitehead
and I worked together to make the numbers more favorable to
get the loan by tweaking the number of seats, the number of

customers expected and the amount that each person would spend.

This was an eye-opening lesson in finance for me. Pro formas are often fictional documents. They are guesses at best. The amount of revenue you expect to make, the number of patrons and how much each one of them will spend, is all entirely speculative. I knew, as did the banker, that I would be able to make it work. I had a good track record of running other restaurants. And with my credit record, and house and cars on the line, they knew that I wouldn't just walk away.

When I got home that day, I went to work, gathering dozens of statements and receipts to prove my credit worthiness. When I was finished, I had a formidable stack of documents. Within a week I dropped off a packet of materials at the bank and waited for the approval or rejection. A month later, Mr. Whitehead called. "Congratulations, your loan has been approved," he said. The following morning, I was the first customer at the bank. When I left an hour and a lot of signatures later, I had a line of credit of $3 million pending finding a location for my concept. With little time to waste, I went to work looking for the perfect place.

Back in the 1940s and '50s, when Washington, DC was still legally segregated, U street was known colloquially as Black Broadway. This was the part of town where Black folks went to the movies, ate at restaurants, got their hair cut, bought a dress or a suit. All levels of people intersected with one another. Black doctors, lawyers, accountants, and business owners mingled with working-class and poor folk. Being next to Howard University made it a hub for Black intellectuals as well as artists, poets, musicians, writers and everyone in between. The Howard Theater opened its doors there in 1910, four years before the

Apollo opened in New York. Without U Street there would have been no Harlem Renaissance. Decades later the area became the epicenter of the civil rights movement in Washington, DC, and, some would argue, the entire country.

However, the riots that were sparked by the assassination of Martin Luther King Jr. in 1968 sent U Street into a downward spiral. The corner of 14th and U was the first to go up in flames when King was killed. The rest of U Street was soon on fire, as was 14th Street, H Street and other commercial corridors. In the wake of the uprising, many Black professionals who lived in the area moved to the suburbs for safety and for better schools. Except for Ben's Chili Bowl and Lee's Flowers, hardly any businesses survived the '68 riots. When I was growing up in the '70s the area had pretty much become a no-go zone. Unless you were looking for hookers or drugs you had no business being there. When I was in high school, a frequent pastime was driving to DC and circling the blocks around U Street to gawk out of the window at the women in stiletto heels and hot pants. During the crack epidemic in the '80s, the area got even worse. The place was deserted after dark.

Things stagnated for a couple of decades in the neighborhood and then there was the upheaval that came with digging tunnels and tearing down streets and sidewalks for the Metro Green Line. It wasn't until the mid-'90s that things began to turn around. By the time I was looking for my space in 2003, several newly constructed apartment buildings were well underway. The Ellington, named after The Duke himself, was one such new luxury development with all the high-end amenities including a common area with plush furniture, a concierge, a gym, stainless steel appliances and granite-top kitchen counters. The rents were at the top end of the market. On the first floor there were storefronts for new businesses. On one end was a bank, on the other a tanning salon. At first I thought the salon was a joke. What an odd choice for a business located in a building named after a famous Black composer and band leader on a street once named Black Broadway. I am not sure if it was an oversight or just outright arrogance, but whatever it was, it didn't fit. Not surprisingly, the tanning salon closed its doors within six months after opening.

I could see that the area was already improving and that, given its history, made me think that U Street was the right area for opening the sort of progressive political space I had in mind. One of the first buildings I considered was the Bohemian Caverns at the corner of 11th and U Street. The Caverns, as it was known, was a three-story standalone with a lighted curved awning resembling a grand piano keyboard. The lights frequently flickered and half of them were always burnt out. I had driven by it several times and wondered what was inside. Mostly it looked abandoned.

The cavern part was just that. You walked through an intricately carved wooden door, down a narrow staircase, and into a dimly lit basement with walls and a ceiling made of faux stone with plastic stalagmites and stalactites resembling those in an underground cave complete with a musty smell. It was a claustrophobic time warp. In the center sat a small, slightly raised stage surrounded by dime-size cocktail tables with tablecloths and chairs just about big enough for a child or a skinny model with no ass. Next to the stage was a grand piano sitting underneath a cave overhang. It was an odd space with poor acoustics and sight-lines, but it was one that packed a lot of history. An impressive roster of jazz greats had played there including Duke Ellington, Ella Fitzgerald, Lena Horne and Nancy Wilson.

The owner, Saed, was an Iranian who had bought the building a few years previously and didn't know exactly what to do with it. Mostly he was renting out the two top floors to clubs and DJ's for private blowouts. The cavern part was used for occasional jazz performances. I made an offer to buy the space and after a few days of haggling, we agreed on a rather shaky deal. Saed turned out to be what is known in the business as a piece of work. He missed appointments, didn't answer calls and made me feel like he was doing me a huge favor when saying things like, "You're stealing this building from me," or "$3 million is nothing for this place." He would swear up and down on his mother's life that he paid more to renovate the building than he did to buy it, letting me know how much he would be losing by selling to me. I didn't believe any of it but continued to humor him to inch the deal along. After several weeks of negotiations, he reluctantly accepted the $3 million offer. It was more than I wanted to spend, but I figured it would pay off over time. I was already pre-approved for the amount having gone through the SBA 540 loan program, which is the type of loan that helps businesses to own the real estate in which they operate. The building would be used as collateral and the loan is guaranteed by the SBA thus allowing banks to take a larger risk. It is one of the best ways to ensure long-term success for a business.

Once I had a signed contract, I went about getting the funds and transferring the money into an escrow account. Even though I went through all the necessary steps to get to the finish line, my gut told me that the deal wasn't going to happen. Saed was shadier than a tropical jungle. On the day of settlement I discovered he had showed up early to the attorney's office. I knew this because by the time I got there he was already leaving. We crossed paths in the elevator, I was heading up and he was on his way down. When the elevator door opened, my attorney was waiting… My attorney was waiting at his office door with a look of astonishment on his face.

"Your seller just walked out," he informed me.

"What do you mean walked out?" I asked, not totally surprised.

"He just got up and left. He walked into the conference room, told me that his wife didn't want to go through with the deal and then he was gone."

Having gone to all the trouble of securing the funds and transferring the money, I was seriously annoyed. I had even shaved for the occasion.

"You can sue him," my lawyer suggested.

Although at the moment my emotions agreed, I knew that suing is time-consuming and costly and would divert my energy away from my ultimate goal. I decided to chalk it up as a lesson learned. Sometimes the universe conspires to tell you something. And it was on me for not paying attention.

Once the moment passed, my indignation quickly turned to relief. In the back of my mind, the Bohemian Caverns was not ideal anyway. Buying a building with such a notable history gave little wiggle room for creativity. The Caverns had been owned by Duke Ellington back in the 40s. It was too much history to get out from under. The broker was upset, of course. He was about to get his payday, and the rug was pulled from under him. But he did what any good broker would do: dusted off his jacket and got back to work. He didn't waste any time. By the end of the day, he had another location to show me.

At the corner of 14th and V Street was a construction site surrounded by a large wooden structure plastered with advertisements of attractive couples feeding each other strawberries, a woman walking her dog, someone on a skateboard. The name of the development was The Langston Lofts. It comprised 80 condo units with two retail bays on the first floor. The building was just beginning to come out from the ground. The first floor was already framed out and a second floor was about to begin.

We peered through the wooden fence. It looked promising. The next day I scheduled a time to meet with the owner, Scott, and walk the site.

Scott's office was in a swanky building near Logan Circle, a few blocks away from the project. A handsome man in his forties with an athletic physique and graying hair, he reeked of privilege and arrogance. He wore straight-legged jeans, a baby blue polo shirt and sockless penny loafers. He leaned back into his leather seat with arms crossed behind his head and legs spread open, taking up as much space as humanly possible. When I told him that what I had in mind for the location included a bookshop, he scoffed.

"Do people still read?" he asked sarcastically, swiveling his chair from side to side.

By the end of the 30-minute meeting I wasn't feeling at all positive about him. We politely shook hands and parted ways. As we left, I turned to my broker and said, "I wouldn't rent from that man if he owned the last building on earth." And I meant it. The broker admonished me not to take it personally. "That's just Scott," he said. But leasing involves a long-term relationship, and I couldn't imagine it working out with someone like Scott. The arrangement would be doomed from the get-go. Rather than dwell on it, I turned my energy to look for other spots.

Two days later, the broker called me. "Can we meet?" he asked. When we got together at Utopia on U Street, he told me "I think there's a way to make this deal with Scott." I was all ears. Scott had shown some interest in selling the space rather than leasing it. He was facing financial pressure and needed to get cash quickly to finish another project that was underway. Having been burned before over the Bohemian Caverns deal, I was reluctant to enter another dead-end deal. Nonetheless, I decided to make an offer to purchase the space. I knew this was a perfect location for what I intended on doing, and buying the space would release me from having to deal with Scott and his outsized ego.

The broker went back and forth but after a couple of rounds we struck a deal. Despite his arrogance, Scott, unlike Saed, was a man of his word. And so, in July of 2004, I bought the first floor of the Langston Lofts at 2021 14th Street NW. It was to become the first Busboys and Poets.

18

THE "BUSBOY POET"

Having seen the disconnect customers had with the tanning spa at the base of the Ellington, I wondered if any of the new residents of the Langston Lofts—named after Langston Hughes, the leading poet of the Harlem Renaissance—knew who Langston was. I was thinking about what to name the new space I was opening, and I decided to make sure it would be linked to the man himself.

The name Busboys and Poets came to me one day while sitting at Jammin' Java in Vienna, Virginia, sipping my bottomless coffee and munching on warm pretzels with Dijon mustard. It was my Saturday routine after dropping off my daughters for piano practice a few blocks away. I looked forward to those precious two hours of solitude, good coffee and pretzels.

I spent the next few weeks going for a deep dive into the world of Langston Hughes. I wanted to know everything about him. I had studied him back in high school, but since then hadn't given his work much thought. This time, I wanted to feel his presence close by. I began by reading the *Collected Poems* edited by Arnold Rampersad, his most respected biographer. He was a Pulitzer finalist for his work on Hughes. Then I devoured Hughes' memoirs *The Big Sea* and *I Wonder As I Wander*. I read each of them twice, once for a quick take and a second time with a highlighter. Much of his memoir is taken up with details of his travels, often facilitated by working on ships. He had an insatiable appetite for discovering the world and using it to find himself. He visited faraway places such as Moscow, Azerbaijan and Iran. I learned about his complicated relationship with his father, who was unable to coexist with the racism he endured in this country, opting to divorce Langston's mother, move to Mexico and marry a Mexican woman. Much of what Hughes writes about is centered on the racism he faced as a Black man living in America in the early part of the 20th century. Traveling across the Mississippi to visit his father in Mexico, he reflected on the endless stream of men and women who were sold to slavery and sent downriver. It moved him to write one of his first, and most important, poems: *The Negro Speaks of Rivers.*

> I've known rivers:
> I've known rivers ancient as the world and older than the flow
>   of human blood in human veins.
> My soul has grown deep like the rivers.
> I bathed in the Euphrates when dawns were young.
> I built my hut near the Congo and it lulled me to sleep.
> I looked upon the Nile and raised the pyramids above it.
> I heard the singing of the Mississippi when Abe Lincoln went
>   down to New Orleans, and I've seen its muddy bosom
>   turn all golden in the sunset.
> I've known rivers:
> Ancient, dusky rivers.
> My soul has grown deep like the rivers.

Reading around in his *oeuvre*, I came across the story of the time he spent in DC. He worked in a variety of odd jobs but found that they often got in the way of his writing. In November 1924, while working as a busboy at the Wardman Park Hotel, a chance encounter with a customer, the well-known American poet Vachel Lindsey, changed his life. Langston recognized him as soon as he sat down. Hastily, he wrote three of his poems on a small piece of paper and placed them next to Lindsey's plate. Lindsey picked up the poems, read them to himself and nodded approvingly. Langston stood at a distance watching. The next morning on his way to work, Langston picked up a copy of the *Evening Star* newspaper, and much to his surprise, saw an article about Lindsey's visit to DC and his discovery of a "busboy poet." He rushed to the hotel, and upon his arrival, was met with a gaggle of photographers who wanted to meet him and take his picture. One of the most iconic photographs is that of Langston Hughes in full whites, carrying a neatly stacked tray of dishes.

At first, I thought the name Busboys and Poets would be too esoteric for the place I wanted to create. I was uncertain whether people would understand what it was all about. After all, it didn't have the words café or restaurant or anything depicting an eating establishment. For weeks I mulled over various alternatives: The Busboy Poet, Busboys and Poets Café, The Poets Café, Café Busboys and Poets. None of them felt right.

I tried out the name Busboys and Poets on different people and got mixed results. Everyone liked the story behind it, but only a few the name itself. It was confusing to most people, often eliciting a head tilt. I shared the idea with Deborah Menkhart, the executive director of a group called Teaching for Change. Deborah is a no-nonsense middle-aged white woman with impeccable integrity and an eagle eye for anything out of place when it comes to social or racial justice. She responded forcefully. "You may want to rethink that," she said. "The word busboy bothers me. The 'boy' part is problematic, particularly if you are looking to be inclusive." I was taken aback. I hadn't thought of that concern. Perhaps she was right.

I turned to others to get their thoughts. I spoke with Ethelbert Miller, a poet and a literary activist. He was on the board of both TFC and the Institute for Policy Studies (IPS) and I respected his perspective greatly. Being Black himself, he assured me that the word "busboy" was not offensive to Black folk, no more than the word cowboy was. When Dean Richardson from Howard University and the award-winning author Marita Golden concurred, I decided to go for it, Busboys and Poets felt bold and confident. The name was decided. Eventually Deborah came around.

I hired Jessie, a graphic designer, to create the logo. I spent days deciding whether to use the word "and" rather than an ampersand. I was concerned that a well-established bookstore in the area already used an ampersand on their signage. I didn't want to be mistaken for them. Jessie was not easy to work with. He was brilliant but also stubborn as hell. I kept reminding him that I was paying him to do the job, and not the other way around. We argued about everything: which fonts to use, whether to put the AND sideways, the colors to be used. But in the end, when Jessie came up with what he insisted was the final version, I loved it immediately. It had an unfinished, edgy feel that looked just right and gave it a "work in progress" look. Our collaboration had paid off.

19

COOKING WITH GAS

By the spring of 2005, with construction well underway, I started spending more and more time inside the space. I'd arrive late in the afternoon after the workers went home and sit on a paint bucket in a corner, taking in the feel of the place. I'd count the passersby on the street outside who, back then, were few and far between and not necessarily people I'd want to see inside. Sitting alone in the dark, I would close my eyes and summon the spirits of the ancestors that filled this corner of the city. The poets, the writers, the musicians, the artists who once occupied these streets. I wanted to get out of the way and let them guide me. Over the weeks the spirits and I grew fond of one another and were mutually comforting. I assured them that I would try to do right by them.

The space was a 7,000-square-foot cold, dark shell. In one corner sat a three-foot-high concrete bump. It had to be there to allow for higher clearance for the underground parking lot beneath the building. It measured about 30 by 20 feet and was an eyesore. For a while I wanted to make it disappear by just building around it and turning it into a storage space or an office. My architect, however, had other plans. A Japanese man with impeccable style, he wore silk suits and ties to match and shoes that gleamed and looked like they never saw a speck of dust. He advised me to consider making a feature of it rather than hiding it.

"Never cover up a flaw if at all possible," he advised.

It's what the Japanese call *kintsugi*: Flaws found in pottery that make it unique and special, rendering the piece far more valuable than the perfect ones. So, out of the unsightly bump, the Langston Hughes Stage emerged. It was the perfect size. Today, it has seen thousands of performances and poetry events, including appearances by some of the most accomplished poets in the world as well as Pulitzer Prize-winning authors, activists, politicians and even Nobel laureates. It became a prototype for the stages that are a major feature at all Busboys and Poets locations.

The next few months were spent meeting people and community members to share my vision of the place. I had learned from my previous experience with Skewers to avoid a situation in which the ideas were swimming in my head, and in my head alone. This time I wanted the world to know well ahead of time what was happening. I needed to create a buzz. When those doors opened, I wanted to see a line of people waiting to get in. There was a lot of suspense about what was happening in this area. U Street was club central, and the community was averse to one more late-night venue bringing noise and trash to a neighborhood that was becoming more and more residential. When people heard about the bookstore and free Wi-Fi, they had little reason to stand in the way. Rather than opposing us, they became advocates, telling their friends and constituents about the cool place that was opening in their neighborhood.

Once in a while, during the months of construction, I invited a friend for a VIP tour. Often those visits were met with a congenial deference. V Street was a sketchy street back in 2004 and 2005 when the first Busboys and Poets was under development. In fact, the V Street block between 13th and 14th was lined with row houses that doubled as crack depots. Drug dealers sat in the porches and cars drove by slowly or double-parked for a quick run.

After several months of construction, the sprint to opening day soon became a crawl. Just when I thought I'd reached the light at the end of the tunnel, it turned out to be an oncoming train. There were so many bumps to negotiate: Licenses. Inspections. Re-inspections. The DC Regulatory Administration, DCRA. Even the mention of the acronym sucks the life out of any entrepreneurial spirit. It was a daily struggle to keep self-doubt from creeping in.

With each inspection, I crossed my fingers and prayed to whatever deity would listen. Sometimes it was a quick review and a simple approval. Sometimes it was much more involved and required days or even weeks to resolve. Luck plays a big role. So much depends on the inspector's mood, what they ate for breakfast, their family situation and other variables out of my control. None of them seem to care or be aware that for a small business, a few days of delay could cost a fortune and mean the difference between success and failure.

By the beginning of July 2005, things were beginning to look less scary. With just a few minor things to attend to, I decided to set Monday August 29, 2005 as the opening date. That would give me enough lead time to hire the staff and take care of small details that still needed attention.

During the weeks leading up to the opening, I had plenty to keep me busy: setting up systems and workflows, preparing inventory sheets, ordering paper products, small wares for the kitchen.

Once our door opened to customers, I would have plenty else to worry about. But I still had to face the most important decision of all: hiring staff. With a few weeks until opening, it was time to start the hiring.

Hiring the right chef was top priority. Without good food and a well-run kitchen, the place would quickly fall apart. Over the years I had observed that people can sometimes tolerate bad service and are willing to give the place a second chance as long as the food is good.

I interviewed about a dozen applicants. One of them, a young woman named Brie, had done stints at some serious restaurants in New York and San Francisco, moving up the ranks to become a first-line cook, the highest level below sous-chef. She impressed me with her culinary knowledge. She had recently moved to the area and wanted to make a name for herself. She specialized in vegan cooking. I wanted the menu to be eclectic, ranging over meat and vegetarian dishes but the thought of having a first-rate vegan chef was exciting. Vegan food was making a stir in some DC restaurants, and I wanted to be in the mix.

I invited Brie back the next day to "stage," a term used for a trial when hiring a chef or a cook, much like an audition. "Just be creative," I told her. She came prepared with her knives and a bag full of ingredients to show off her skills. I watched from behind the line as she expertly moved about the kitchen, setting out a couple of clean towels and laying out her knives in order of size. She arranged the ingredients on a cutting board: tofu, coconut shavings, and soy milk. Next, she reached into her bag of goodies and took out a few hand-labeled Mason jars that contained different sauces. She laid thick blocks of tofu on a cutting board and carefully cut them into equal-sized cubes. She then set up three pans, into which she would dip each tofu cube: first, a soy milk bath; second, flour for dredging; and last, coconut shavings to coat the outside. Meanwhile she poured some oil into a shallow pan, turned up the heat and let it smoke a little. I watched her drop the coated cubes into the oil, turning them delicately one by one, making sure that all sides were perfectly golden. She then placed them on a paper towel to cool off slightly. When they were done, she arranged them into a pyramid on a plate and drizzled a peppery honey sauce with flecks of chili peppers. She carried the dish, making sure the pyramid stayed intact, and placed it in front of me. I took one bite, and I was blown away. The crunch of the tofu crust, the savory-sweet balance, the heat from the chili; it all worked. Brie knew how to cook, no doubt about that.

"Chefing" is not just about cooking; it also requires leadership skills. Organization. Ability to motivate. Ability to withstand the heat, literally and figuratively, when things don't go as planned. The ability to produce the same dish over and over again and get it right every time. Much like a Broadway actor who has to perform the exact same role for months, maybe even years, and make it seem fresh and exciting every time. And the last thing, most important of all, you have to know your audience. The customers who pay your salary. The actual boss, without whom you are the tree that falls in the forest where no one is there to hear you.

It was here that an insurmountable problem presented itself with Brie. It emerged that she was not interested in preparing non-vegan dishes; indeed, the idea of cooking with meat and dairy was stomach-churning for her. Back in 2005, a tiny percentage of people were actually vegan; few even knew what it meant. Brie's menu, delicious as it was, would leave out 99% of the community that Busboys and Poets intended to reach. I let her know that her dishes were spectacular, but they would not serve this place well. In a sense she knocked it out of the park, and not in a good way. For a moment I even thought about opening another restaurant and calling it "Brie's." I hated to lose her. But I knew it would be impossible trying to fit this circle into a square.

To save time and avert another disaster, I decided to go for the tried and tested. The sous-chef at Mimi's, Hugo, had shown some impressive potential. What he lacked in creativity, he made up in consistency. He was as dependable as a Swiss clock. And ambitious to boot. At the age of eight he had made his way by crossing the Rio Grande with his family, and, like many El Salvadorians, he started working in kitchens in DC, where they finally settled. He went from dishwasher to prep cook and then, on the line, he worked his way up to head cook. He learned most of his skills by jumping in when needed, making himself invaluable to any kitchen and watching the more seasoned cooks, who were all too happy to help him.

When I offered him the job he was ecstatic at the new challenge. I would be collaborating closely with him to create a menu that was simple, spirited, and easy to understand and pronounce. With little time to waste, we went to work right away, creating a menu that was accessible and in line with the Busboys and Poets mission. Having worked with me for nearly two years, he immediately got what I was looking for: a modern, Southern-focused menu. Within the span of a couple of days he was ready to take a stab at a tasting. His food, although not the *haute cuisine* created by Brie, still managed to impress. It was a walk down memory lane of the top hits from Café Luna, Luna Grill & Diner and Mimi's, a nice mix covering all tastes and dietary needs. The menu included a vegetarian spinach lasagna with a bechamel sauce, a meatloaf with a charred ketchup glaze and mashed potatoes, and a pan-seared catfish with a corn cake and collards, which quickly became a big hit. The corn cakes were made to order with chunks of corn and a jalapeño kick. There was a nice variety of sandwiches including a thick grilled cheese with bacon on sourdough bread and an eight-ounce grass-fed burger on a brioche bun that rivaled any high-end hotel restaurant, plus a handful of salads: Cobb, spinach with fruit, falafel and Caesar. I even added a peanut butter and banana sandwich with agave instead of honey to make it 100 percent vegan. Working closely with Hugo, I made sure there were good options for vegetarians and vegans. Brie's coconut tofu bites also made the cut. I wanted to make sure we used the best ingredients possible. I shopped around for purveyors who specialized in local and organic products. I took a day trip to visit farms and co-ops in southern Pennsylvania to get the best deals. Now, with the chef hired, and the menu well underway, we were "cooking with gas," as Daniel used to say.

With a large event space to fill, I needed someone dynamic and organized to manage the events we would be hosting. They had to be a person who would understand the mission of the place, making sure that the programming represented the community we were serving. Poetry would be a major feature in our calendar. Political events would also be a priority. Book talks and panel discussions would have to be carefully selected to reinforce the fusion of art, culture and politics. The panels would need to focus on issues of race, culture and social justice. If the kitchen was the heart of the sort of restaurant I wanted to create, then the events would be its soul, breathing life within its walls. That's why, next to the chef, the events and marketing manager would be the most important person in the new set-up. In later years this position would be elevated to the VP level. Vibe Protector.

Pamela Pinnock had applied to work as a salesclerk at the bookstore that was to be a part of the new order. She had previously worked at Borders Books. The manager of the bookstore mentioned to me that she might be a good fit for the events position, and so I interviewed her. A tall Black woman with short natural hair and a voice that rang with confidence, Pamela made an immediate impression. She had deep, progressive politics, with a view of the world that was sophisticated and nuanced. She understood intersectionality and knew that the struggle of Black people in southeast DC was linked to the struggle of Palestinians or other oppressed peoples anywhere in the world. Busboys was going to be representative of progressive American values. Not Black, not white. American. I didn't have to explain it to her. She knew exactly what I was talking about. We frequently completed each other's sentences.

Pamela was excited at the opportunity. She was single and had just been through a rough patch in her work life. Her home improvement business had gone belly up. She was neck-deep in debt and needed to get back on her feet. The timing and the match couldn't have been better. She plunged right in, making an inventory of various art and culture groups in the area. In a single day she came up with ideas and events that would span an entire year of programming. We met every afternoon thereafter, sometimes for hours, coming up with a list of possible events. She began contacting non-profits all over the city, introducing Busboys and Poets to them. She and the bookstore manager drew up a list of authors that we wanted to feature. It included Howard Zinn, Angela Davis, Alice Walker, Amy Goodman, Cindy Sheehan (the anti-war activist whose son in the U.S. Army was killed in Iraq), Cornel West and dozens more. She also made an inventory of local authors and writers and another one of major political figures that might be invited. Definitely not Colin Powell or Hillary Clinton, we both agreed.

With the kitchen on solid footing and the events and program-ming underway, I hired a manager to oversee day-to-day oper-ations. Again, I decided to go with a sure thing. Mark was the front house manager at Mimi's at the time and needed a change. I decided he would oversee the front of the house. He was reliable and committed. I worked closely with him to set up systems for servers, bartenders, bussers, food run-ners, playing out different scenarios and workflows. I placed an ad in several local papers for the front-of-house positions and held several open houses. By the end of the week we had interviewed well over 100 people and hired our opening crew of 15. Then Mark and the new hires got to work setting up the dining room, numbering the tables, assigning sections, mak-ing opening and closing checklists and programming the POS system. As opening day drew near, we were ready, or at least we thought we were.

A few weeks before opening, Dave Zirin, a friend and author who writes about the intersection of politics and sports, con-tacted me with an idea. He wanted to interview Etan Thomas, the center forward for the local basketball team, the Washington Wizards, before a live audience on stage in the Langston Room. He had visited me and was excited about the possibility of using the space for such an event. I was thrilled by the idea. Thomas was a gifted poet and a committed activist, as well as a superb athlete. Having him be the first poet on opening day on the Langston Hughes stage would be a real coup, setting the tone for future events.

As the day of the event drew near, it was becoming more and more obvious that we would not be able to open in time. Too many unforeseeable things were popping up left and right, but I didn't want to cancel or postpone. By then, the build-out was already completed. The stage was finished, lights were installed, and a great sound system was ready to go. The furniture was already in place. Even the salt and pepper shakers were filled. All we needed were one or two final inspections to open to the public.

Canceling would have been a real bummer. Many people had already heard about the event and I didn't want to lose the momentum, knowing that buzz is an important element in restaurants. After weighing the options, I decided to go ahead despite the risk involved. Technically I was doing little wrong, since no food or beverages were to be served. But if the city found out, it could mean a fine and possibly more delays. We would have to hold the event on the down-low.

That night, I closed all the curtains to the outside, dimmed the lights, crossed my fingers and had the Langston Room readied for hosting its first public event, candles and all. I had someone stand at the front door directing people to the back door. People started to trickle in through the kitchen. Within minutes, the Langston Room was full to capacity with barely enough standing room. I kept my eye on the front door in case a nosy neighbor peeked in.

The event started with a conversation between Dave and Etan. Once the interview part was over, it was time for Etan to do his thing. His 6'7" frame towered over Dave. He flipped his long dreads to one side, adjusted the mic and began his poetry set. The crowd was rapt, snapping and calling back, hooting and hollering with sprinkles of mmm's and ahhh's. When the event was over, people stayed to talk and connect with old friends. Although this was not a formal opening, it was exciting to see what future events would look like. The stage, the lights, the mics. Everything worked perfectly. And I started to imagine the possibilities.

One of the most important elements that has come to define Busboys and Poets is the bookstore, carrying titles that are heavily skewed toward people of color. Titles that are often left out at conventional bookstores. Having run a bookstore previously, I knew the amount of work it took to manage and keep up with new titles, placing orders, managing returns. The amount of paperwork is enormous. There are catalogs to review, authors to reach out to and confirm, shelves to fill, shrinkage to monitor. Having someone else take all this on would save me a great deal of headache.

Teaching for Change (TFC) was the ideal partner. A local non-profit, its mission is as follows: "To provide teachers and parents with the tools to create schools where students learn to read, write, and change the world." They help schools revamp their curricula, to make them representative racially and ethnically with an eye on social justice. Around the opening time of Busboys and Poets I sat on their board of directors. Every year TFC would put out a catalog of upcoming recommended books and authors who were on the forefront of social change. I used to look forward to getting the listing of these books and circling the ones I wanted. I would fill out the form and mail it in with a check and sit back and wait for the box of books to arrive. What a treat it was when it came to the door. I would spend the entire day leafing through the new titles.

During one board meeting I suggested the idea that the bookstore at Busboys and Poets should be run by TFC. I made them an offer they couldn't refuse. I would build out the entire space, shelves, counters and all. All TFC had to do was to purchase the books and hire the staff. All sales and profits went directly to them. They would pay no rent nor have any other expenses. It was a handshake deal. I was thrilled when the board voted unanimously to approve the bookstore operation. And for the following ten years they managed the bookstore magnificently.

20

THE MURAL

The two Black women peering through a crack in the paper that we had used to cover the windows of the new restaurant lingered longer than most. They were dressed as if going to church, right down to their hats, stockings, and chunky-heeled shoes. One wore a tan coat, the other a brown one, clutching a purse at her side. They were searching for an opening in the paper, a rip, to take a peek at what was inside. There were no "coming soon" or "now hiring" posters. There was no signage displaying the name. I knew that what we were creating would cause a stir and I wanted to unveil it at the right moment.

For the past few weeks, passersby regularly tried to get a glimpse inside, but these two women were more persistent, walking back and forth to find the largest opening in the paper for the best view. They cupped their hands against the window, searching for clues. I stepped outside and quickly invited them in. "Are you from around here?" I asked. "I'm a fourth-generation Washingtonian," said the one with the tan coat. "I'm sixth-generation," the other added proudly. "Thank you for stopping by," I said.

This was their community, and they were curious about the types of businesses that were filling the once-empty storefronts. They had seen previous transformations of the neighborhood. They had lived through it all: segregation, riots, the crack epidemic, nightly gunshots. And now, decades later, they were seeing another round of change.

Once inside, the two women continued surveying the space as if they were lunar landers analyzing samples of the terrain. They took note of the couches and communal seating arrangements, the heavily stocked bar, the artwork, the well-lit lounge and the bookstore with stacked titles from Langston Hughes, Gil Scott-Heron, Howard Zinn, Toni Morrison and Alice Walker.

"Who's the owner?" the one with the purse asked.

"I am," I replied cheerfully.

"Mmm."

After a few awkward moments the other asked, "Where you from?"

"I'm originally from Iraq," I said. "Baghdad."

I knew that the answer I gave was not the one they were looking for. They wanted to hear that I was Black. A brother. One of them. Like the girl with the pleated skirt at Stratford Junior High, they wanted to know if I was "high yellow."

"I-raq?" the one with the tan coat said, giving me the once-over.

The one with the purse stood quietly.

"You know, the country we just invaded and destroyed," I said sarcastically, then quickly adding, "I've lived here most of my life though."

"What's this place going to be?" one of them continued without looking at me, adjusting her floral hat and pulling her purse closer to her body as if shielding herself from what I was about to say.

"It's a community space with a restaurant, bar, Wi-Fi and a theater space for poetry and author events," I said.

My comments were met mostly with awkward "hmm's," "aah's" and "oh's."

"Let me show you the back room," I said, leading them further down the long, tiled hallway.

Although I was trying to appear confident, my heart was pounding. I was about to show them the soul of the restaurant, a large performance space that could seat up to 80 people in front of the stage we had built, complete with professional lights and a concert-quality sound system. Over the years that followed, this stage would be home to some of the most significant activists, writers and poets, giants like Ralph Nader, Angela Davis, Alice Walker, Joan Baez, Jesse Jackson, Rigoberta Menchu and so many others. While listening to these speakers and poets you could at the same time be nourishing yourself with a bowl of lentil soup, Howard Zinn's favorite, or catfish with grits, of which Cornel West once said, "Brother Andy, this is the best catfish I've ever had." This is not just *any* restaurant, it is a place with a "tribal statement": Busboys and Poets is a place where you can feed your mind, body and soul, all in the same visit. I held my breath and threw open the double French doors. "This," I announced, "is the Langston Room, named after the great poet Langston Hughes."

The women stood still, surveying the room, their attention fixed on the large mural straight ahead, which I had made. The idea for it came from Colman McCarthy, a pacifist and longtime columnist for the *Washington Post*. He often spoke about how most Americans can name presidents and generals but have little knowledge about activists and the real changemakers. I had labored over it for weeks. It depicts the civil rights struggles of the past century. I had found black and white photographs of the heroes of such movements, enlarged them at a nearby Kinko's, and then wheat pasted them onto the wall. Once they were dry, I used sandpaper to blend the portraits with the background and then painted the edges with sepia colored paint to give the impression of layers of images. I added words using a grease pencil and then sealed the whole wall with polyurethane mixed with a few drops of brown paint to give the images a muted antique look.

I had taken particular care not to leave out any major moments in the history of the civil rights struggle, making sure that the lesser-known heroes and sheroes were represented. I wanted the mural to be both an educational piece and visual statement that showed what Busboys and Poets was all about. I remembered what Howard Zinn had told me: it's not the history you tell that matters, it's the history you leave out.

At the center of the mural are portraits of two giants of civil rights, Martin Luther King, Jr., and Mahatma Gandhi. But close by is the much lesser-known Jeanette Rankin, the first woman to hold national elected office in 1917 and the lone vote in Congress against World War I. She said at the time, "I wish to stand for my country, but I cannot vote for war." She was defeated when she ran for a second term. Years later when, as fate would have it, America was readying to enter another world war, she ran again and won. Once again Rankin voted against the war, stating her position as before. When I first learned about this remarkable woman, I was surprised that she was paid so little attention in the telling of our history. Placing her prominently in the mural was a small contribution to putting that right. Then there is Jodie Williams, who led a campaign to abolish land mines. Shirin Abadi, the Iranian attorney and human rights activist. There is young Ralph Nader, who single-handedly started more than 100 consumer protection organizations. In large part, we have him to thank for the Freedom of Information Act, whistleblower protection laws, seat belts, clean water, clean air and food labeling, to name a few. Kwame Ture is up on the wall too, and so is Rosa Parks. Years later I added Bob Marley on his birthdate, facing John Lennon with the words, "one love," connecting them. Both used their celebrity to promote peace and speak up for the silenced. These were images I had grown up with and people and movements that shaped my life. You will not see any generals or presidents or kings on the mural in the Langston Room. It is an homage to peace and justice movements and the people who took part in them.

At the top of the mural, I wrote the first two stanzas of Langston Hughes' epic poem "Let America Be America Again." This was the first poem I memorized in middle school less than a year after my family came to America. It took me weeks to learn it. My goal was to memorize a stanza at a time. I stuck to it, adding one more each day. When I got to the fifth or sixth, I had to repeat them over and over again all day long to hold on to what I memorized. I was obsessed. I repeated them in my head on the way to school. In the cafeteria. In the shower. At home in bed. I didn't know what most of the words meant but having them come out of my mouth made me feel powerful and more confident. Later, when I learned their meaning, the words revealed the complexity of America to me and, with each passing year, the poem has become ever more poignant and relevant:

> Let America be America again.
> Let it be the dream it used to be.
> Let it be the pioneer on the plain
> Seeking a home where he himself is free.
>
> (America never was America to me.)
>
> Let America be the dream the dreamers dreamed–
> Let it be that great strong land of love
> Where never kings connive nor tyrants scheme
> That any man be crushed by one above.
>
> (It never was America to me.)
>
> O, let my land be a land where Liberty

Is crowned with no false patriotic wreath,
But opportunity is real, and life is free,
Equality is in the air we breathe …

The mural has been a focal point of the space and tells a story that words alone could not. Over the years several of the people who appear in it have spoken at Busboys and Poets and were able to sign their name and write a short message on it. I was moved each time that happened. Jesse Jackson signed his name next to his photo, as did Ralph Nader, Alice Walker, Ethelbert Miller, Jodie Williams. Nelson Mandela's daughter, Zindzi, signed her name next to her father's image. Also up on the wall is the SNCC (Student Non-Violence Coordinating Committee) Statement of Purpose, a favorite of mine. It contains words that are so powerful, they give me goosebumps:

Through nonviolence, courage displaces fear; love transforms hate. Acceptance dissipates prejudice; hope ends despair. Peace dominates war; faith reconciles doubt. Mutual regard cancels enmity. Justice for all overcomes injustice. The redemptive community supersedes systems of gross social immorality.

Years after we opened, I watched Congressman John Lewis, once the chairman of the organization, climb the booth below the statement and sign it with a black Sharpie. What an honor that was.

I turned my head slowly to see the expression on the women's faces. One of them had a tear making its way across her cheek. The other was cupping her mouth. It was a moment that I will remember forever. The moment when I realized that I had created a space where uplifting race and culture takes front and center. "This is beautiful," one of them said softly.

"Thank you," I said. "Can I give you a hug?"

They threw their arms out, and we all embraced.

21

OPENING NIGHT

Two years into the war and the promised WMDs were nowhere to be found. The streets were on fire. The lies and deception from the White House and the Pentagon were on full display, but despite the horrors of the ongoing war, a sense of joy and hope also filled the air.

A huge anti-war march was being planned around the end of September 2005. Word on the street was that this was going to be the largest anti-war march in US history. Every peace and justice group had joined the call. United For Peace and Justice, ANSWER Coalition, Code Pink, Military Families Speak Out, environmental groups and so many others, big and small. New organizations and coalitions were forming every day. They met almost nightly at All Souls Church and other venues in DC, planning and strategizing. I made it a point to attend as many of those meetings as I could. Movie stars like Jane Fonda, Tim Robbins and Susan Sarandon were leading the Hollywood contingent.

The seed for Busboys and Poets had been planted in my head around the time of 9/11, back in 2001. It began to germinate at the beginning of the Iraq War in early 2003. And now, in 2005, it was ready to sprout. It was the perfect moment for an opening of this sort of place. I couldn't have planned it better had I tried. A convergence of every imaginable peace group was showing up at my doorstep. Word had gone out about this oddly named new place that was about to open its doors and welcome peace activists. The owner, an Iraqi no less, was an activist himself. If serendipity had a name, it would have been Busboys and Poets.

We opened our doors on September 7, 2005. A Wednesday, two days after Labor Day. I was as surprised as anyone at how quickly the place filled up. Word had evidently traveled fast and wide. I thought back to when I opened my first restaurant in DC, Skewers, and sat at the edge of the bar waiting a long time for the first guests to arrive, trying to remain upbeat. Those days were far behind me. Since then, I had learned about the value of connecting with the community months before opening. Showing up at every Advisory Neighborhood Commission (ANC) gathering, condo association meeting, joining listservs, meeting key community leaders, hiring the right people and sharing the vision with them.

The first night had to be cut short. We ran out of just about everything two hours before the planned closing time. I was exhausted, and so was everyone else. One bartender bending over with both her hands on her knees, panting and completely spent, shouted out, "What a shitshow!" Then she straightened up and high-fived everyone nearby adding, "But we did it!" Glasses were everywhere at the bar, dishes on every surface in the kitchen, staff running ragged with their tongues hanging out. For the next few hours everyone pitched in furiously to put the pieces back together.

I had anticipated a steady stream on the first day, but this was a tsunami, and here I was standing in the middle of its aftermath. With the reception we received the first night, I knew that the next day would be even bigger. We had no time to waste. I had to figure out how to make it less chaotic, and fast. Rearranging things for better workflow. Buying more dishes and silverware. Hiring more staff. I had to change the tires at pit-stop speed.

"What do you think?" Pamela asked with a knowing smile, holding a mop. She had signed up for an administrative job but, like everyone else, was lending a hand in the clean-up.

"I had no idea. I knew it would be busy but not like this," I said.

"I think we have a hit on our hands," she said.

Not wanting to jinx things, I carried on cleaning and held back my response for a moment. "I hope you're right," I said tentatively.

She continued doing figure-eights with the mop. Sweat was running across her forehead.

"Wow!" she said. "What an amazing night. Are you happy?" she asked.

"Happy would be an understatement," I said. "I expected some business, but not like this. This is beyond my wildest dreams."

A little after midnight, everyone was ready to call it a day. Soon, one by one, they left. When the last person said their goodbyes, I locked the front door, turned off the lights, went back to the Langston Room, sat in one of the booths underneath the mural and took a deep breath. I let Marjan know that I would be sleeping at the place. Knowing how obsessive I am, she didn't protest. "Get some rest," she said.

The streetlight bathed the room, casting moving shadows across the mural. I looked around the place and unexpectedly, out of nowhere, a flood of tears rolled down my face. They were triumphant tears that I had been holding back from the moment we opened the door, maybe even before then. It was a joyful night of people who came for dinner or a drink, but also to find community in the midst of turmoil.

Now that I was alone, it was time to exhale. All those years of work and planning had led up to this day, to this place, at this time. From my father's pizza place back in the strip mall in

Annandale, Virginia, until now, I had been preparing for this my entire life. Busboys and Poets was a culmination of decades of community involvement, working in kitchens, waiting tables and bartending, demonstrating, hosting Peace Cafés, joining race talks, working on social justice issues, volunteering for political campaigns, and on and on. It was something that I had dreamed about and held close to my chest, waiting to bring it to light when the time was right. It was a moment that was perhaps too early to savor fully and yet here I was, sitting in the Langston Room, staring at the mural and looking forward to what lay ahead. I wiped the tears off my face with the back of my hand and curled up in the booth using my backpack as a headrest. In a few hours it would be daylight, and I wanted to get an early start. I knew now that I had created something more than a restaurant. Busboys and Poets would be a sanctuary for those who believe that a better world is possible. Not Black, not white, just human beings looking to connect with other like-minded folk. I closed my eyes and slept soundly. I had found my tribe.

To be continued…

ACKNOWLEDGEMENTS

My first shoutout must go to my wife, Marjan, who had to put up with listening to multiple readings of these pages. She is my best and fiercest critic. To my children, Geoffrey, Matthew, Laela and Nina whose friendship and humor I appreciate and cherish. To my brother, Yasir, who is my best friend and someone I can always depend on through thick and thin. To my sister, May, who is the best sounding board. Her wit and sharp retorts keep me on my toes. To my mother, Suad, who at 95 still knows how to laugh and who taught me what it means to be a peacemaker.

A very special thanks goes to the leadership team at Busboys and Poets who continue to do an excellent job, day in and day out. Their dedication and passion is what keeps this company going. It's also what keeps me going. Hicham Baamrani, Robert Ventura, Alisha Byrd, Joy Zarembka, Ramesh Sapkota. And to the people who are on the front line, the staff of Busboys and Poets; the front and back of the house managers, the servers, booksellers, bartenders, directors, administrators, bussers, runners, hosts, cooks, and dishwashers. They make the whole thing look easy.

To Ethelbert Miller, my friend and mentor, for the wisdom and advice that he has given so generously over the years. To Ralph Nader, the most optimistic man I know, who taught me that democracy is not a spectator sport and to continue to fight for the long haul. To Medea Benjamin, who sets the highest bar for what it means to be a patriot and an activist. Her tireless pursuit of truth and justice has inspired me for decades. To James Early, whose perspective and insight into progressive politics has been invaluable. To Dera Tompkins, whose frank conversations over a mimosa and coffee are always eye-opening. To Njoki Njehu, a friend, a comrade, and one who early on showed me that civil disobedience can be a joyful, collective experience. To Dave Zirin for being a part of the Busboys and Poets family early on. To Deborah Menkhart, the ED of Teaching for Change, for her impeccable moral compass and doggedness on issues that matter. To Pamela Pinnock, who is a treasure trove of ideas and who instantly understood the Busboys and Poets mission and became part of its DNA. And to Mary Amato, who helped me think through the structure of the book and give it some order.

To all the poets and artists that are part of the poetry family and especially our past and current DOPS (Poets in Residence), Derick Weston Brown, Pages Matam, Sonya Renee Taylor, and Charity Blackwell. And a special shout out to Charlotte Fox, for helping us to professionalize our poetry program and make it more sustainable. To Carol Dyson, for her commitment to making art a part of social change and for keeping the walls at Busboys and Poets beautifully adorned over the years.

A very special thank you to Gina Dent and Angela Davis, whose intellectual muscle continues to bend the arc of the universe toward justice. To Alice Walker, who holds a special place in my heart and whose support I so appreciate.

And lastly and most importantly, to all the friends and patrons who frequent Busboys and Poets and whose support over the years has kept the lights on.

Thank you!

~~~ of love   Where never kings collusive har~~~
~~~ in this "homeland of the free.")   LANG

you want peace work for justice!

Just say NO to WAR!

PEACE

Peace is hard work

Palestine remains one of
the great moral causes
of our time.....

I think ...
peace so...
of their...
had better...
why an...